REVEALED

True Testimonials and Life Lessons on Covert and Blatant Racial Experiences

DARLENE V. GRIFFIN-WILLIS PH.D.

REVEALED

True Testimonials and Life Lessons on Covert and Blatant Racial Experiences

DARLENE V. GRIFFIN-WILLIS PH.D.

MEWE
Lithonia, GA

Griffin-Willis, Darlene V.
    REVEALED: True Testimonials and Life Lessons on Covert and Blatant Racial Experiences / Darlene V. Griffin-Willis, Ph.D.

ISBN: 978-1-7334383-8-4

Library of Congress Control Number: 2020921404

For Worldwide Distribution
Printed in the USA

This book is dedicated to my nephew, Shawn Edward Washington, II, who left us too soon due to healthcare workers being more concerned about the color of his skin and insurance, rather than the quality of his care.

It is also dedicated to our sweet Aunt Julia Sandifer who was a faithful woman of God and role model for all of us. Her passing symbolized the closing of a chapter for a family generation that will never be forgotten.

Another personal dedication is my late first cousin, Bobbie Jones, who was the best cook with the biggest heart and loved by all. To her two brothers and my first cousins, Lionel "Lonnie" Johnson and Calvin Jones as well as my nephew, Michael Osborne, great niece Kylynn and brother-in-law, Walter Lee Willis, Sr. Even though all of you left us too soon, you continue to leave a mark on this world, especially through your children and loved ones! During the writing of this book, my 41-year-old cousin, Jasmine, passed away. May her beautiful smile and free spirit soar even higher.

I stand on the shoulders of my ancestors reaching back to my great-great-great-grandmother, Maize, to my great-great-grandmother, Armentine, my great-grandparents: Fannie & Joseph Dyels, Georgia "Dee" & Nick Griffin, Mary & Albert Hart, Sr., and my "Mama Mae," aka Mary M. Chambers. My grandparents: Geneva & Rev. James C. Griffin, Sr., Marion L & Jake M. Dyels, Sr.; Mother and Father-in love: Pernola & Phillip Willis, Sr.; Aunts and Uncles: Marguerite "Aunt Bobby" & Albert Hart, Jr, Ollie B. Dyels, Uncle Henry Sandifer, Ben Turner, Floyd Martin, Jake Marion Dyels, Jr., Shirley Ann and James Dyels, Sandra Diane Newton, Shirley Gail Dyels and Sylvia Rochelle Dyels. Sister-in-love Theresa Willis.

To all of my mentors who have transitioned, but made a lasting impact on my life. In fact, I attribute them for helping to shape who I am today. Thank you to the late greats: God Father of Black Psychology, Dr. Joseph L. White; 21st International President for Alpha Kappa Alpha Sorority, Incorporated, Faye B. Bryant; Supervisor/Friend, Joyce Montgomery; 1st and 2nd grade teacher and model, Ms. Leona DeBique; my School Nurse, Mrs. Dolores Warren, and her sister who was a nurse as well, Ms. Mercedes; and my junior high school English teacher, Mrs. Masaye Nakamura, who was the first Japanese American teacher hired by Oakland Public Schools and a survivor during the war when she was forced to leave UCLA to be imprisoned just for being Japanese. She stood less than 5 ft. tall but used her experiences to devote her life to empowering underserved and underrepresented students.

TABLE OF CONTENTS

ACKNOWLEDGEMENTS

As a woman of faith, I always give God the glory for using me as a vessel to touch and/or change countless lives as I fulfill His purpose for me.

To my husband, Phillip Jr., for being supportive behind the scenes for the past 34 years as well as our adult sons, Phillip III and James Cornelius for never leaving my side, especially during the challenging times. I wouldn't have been able to take on this project without your support. Thank you for accepting me on my good and bad days!

To my "Mommie and Daddy," Sheryle and James C. Griffin, Jr., who have been blessed to be married for 60 years. They sacrificed so much for their six daughters and provided us with lots of love and unlimited opportunities. My parents have always believed in me since the day of my birth. The doctor told my Mom that I was dead but she knew that God was in control and refused to give up, telling him, "My baby is not dead!" A few hours later, I was born feet first and still haven't stopped running!!

To my Aunt Joy, Uncle Joel, and Sorority Sister Barbara: Thank you for putting up with my countless calls, allowing me to pick your brains, and leaning on your wisdom and knowledge! I thank God for all of you! Aunt Joy, I am forever thankful for you introducing me to our beloved sorority and for our daily calls of inspiration and venting!

To my five sisters, brother-in-loves, and sister-in-loves who have loved me unconditionally: Thank you Debbie and Arthur, Dawn and Terry, Dana and Charles, Denise and Dianna, Spencer and Ruthie, Beverly and Rev. Eddie, Tony and DeVicki, Leroy, Willie James, Bettye and Johnny, and Magnolia. It is an honor to be related to each of you and I thank God for selecting us as family.

To my aunts and uncles: Aunt Carriel "Auntie", Aunt Sharon, Aunt Doris Jean, Aunt Joanne, Aunt Jeanne, and Uncle Lee. Thank you for being a phone call, text message, or flight away.

To my nieces and nephews: Matthew, Robert, Davon and Katie who are expecting our newest family baby, Alison, Sheryle, Sharon, Dom, Willie

(TJ), Kevin, Trevor, AmandaDawn, Nicole, Nakaia, Kiysha, Tianna, Chucky, Aszanee, Jahnavee, Breauna, Darryl, Walter, Jacquelyn, Dr. Spencer Willis, Jr., Willie (Little Willie), Kristin, Derek, Angela, Tony (TC), and Jon. Great nieces and nephews: Twins Trecee and Maiyah, Taylor, Tashi, Jayla, Railyn, Charles, Jr. (CJ), Jayceon, Aquira, Davari, JaKing, Demetrius, CeAuna, Miracle, and our beautiful Shawnyce who reminds us of her amazing Dad, Shawn E. Wa. Great great nephew, Jionni. You all are the future, and "Auntie Wary/Darlene" supports, loves, and believes in each of you.

To my cousins: "Ken Ken," you started influencing my life years ago by helping me to believe that I could go to college and be whatever I wanted to be; "Lennyboy," you reminded me that I'm overdue to write my second book and you continue to serve as my sounding board as well as loving me unconditionally; Pastor David C. Hartfield-Dyels, you continue to pray for me and help guide me during this book process and life; Robin, who took the time to let me spend time with her at college and helped me get my first college internship; Ton Ton and Gonnyman, for always being a phone call away for their panicking cousin ☺; Dana (a second cousin removed) who immediately responded to my call to the family about this book project because she could identify with the labor involved as she had just worked hard this year to earn her MA and published her project on "Emotional Labor: How Gendered Racism Affects African American Women Working in Mental Health Crisis Response."

To my 34 out of 37 first cousins that are still here with us on earth: Thank you for working hard to continue making a difference: Voncelle, Eugene, Regenia, Linda, Senvia, Donna, Dwight, Jocelyn, Karen, Janice, Kevin, Moria, Mako, Joel (Jojo), Jerome (Romey), Mia, Little Ben, Lance (Bimbo), Len (Lennyboy), Lagon (Gonnyman), Leland (T-Babe), LaTanya (Ton-Ton), Deone, Dereck, Danielle, Denise, Juanita, Jamie, David Charles, Sylvia, David Leonard, Michael, Drena, and Francis. Thank you for being my first cousins who never judge but are there for me unconditionally.

To my Pastor Victor Brice & Mrs. Tara Brice and Rev. Samuel Brice & Alisa Harris-Brice: Thank you for praying for me during my health challenges, always being there for our family, and your willingness to encourage the college bound programs to be expanded into churches. You constantly remind me that God is soooo good!

To my College Bound scholars and families whom we've served for almost 20 years! It has been and continues to be my honor to serve and empower each and every one of you. Thanks for being open to working hard to successfully navigate the educational system and having the choice of attending college! I'm so proud of each and every one of you!

Special thanks to "Nita Painter" with the San Diego NAACP–ACT SO, who listens to the weekly "Scholarship Sundays with Dr. Dary" empowerment program. We asked all the viewers to participate in a title competition and she suggested the title REVEALED! After much prayer, I decided to go with this title and create a subtitle that followed. Thank you so much Nita... you are awesome!

To the beautiful women of Alpha Kappa Alpha Sorority, Incorporated. I joined this amazing sorority over 37 years ago and it was one of the best decisions I could have made.

To my longtime friends who are like family and often serve as my sounding board, Sharon, Soncia, Michael, Marilyn, Gary, Sandy, Linda, Tony, Toby, Darryl, Marsha, Martha, Catherine, Mae, Renee, Ashanti, Lisa, Sheila, Claire, Beverly, Joey, Darrell, Brenda, Jackie, Osceola, Michelle, Joe, Hjordis, Uncle Fred and Aunt Bonnie plus countless others who are always a phone call or text message away. A special shout out to my scholars who have worked hard to earn their professional titles, Briana, Kiara, Ashley and Erin.

To our family friends who have known me since I was a little girl! No, we don't talk everyday but I just know that I can call them anytime I need anything. Thank you Mr. and Mrs. McWilliams, Mr. and Mrs. Bellow, Ms. Troupe, Mrs. Joan Lewis, Ms. Borens, Ms. Bowles, Aunt Nancy, Ms. Maroney, Ms. Simms, and Mrs. Green.

*Special thanks to Mr. Ben Carrasco! Thanks for helping to kick off the first **Revealed** book cover (beyondthelens@gmail.com).*

To my 6:30 am daily prayer Sistahs: Ms. Rubee, Dana, Alison, Tracy, LeAne and Pam. Look at God and yes we know that prayer works!!!

Thank you to the dynamic team that helped work behind the scenes! You know who you are!

Specials thanks to my Sorority Sister, Charlotte Dudley, who was referred to me by my cousin David Charles Hartfield-Dyels. Thanks for taking my call as I panicked due to life getting in the way! If you need a publisher, please consider MEWE out of Atlanta, Georgia. She is God-sent! Contact her at mewecorporation@gmail.com.

Last but certainly not least, to all of the people that took the time to complete the systemic racism survey within a two-week deadline! Many put your lives on hold just to respond back to my request understanding that together we would be providing true testimonials that have the potential to help others and be used as an exchange of dialogue regarding courageous conversations!

THE PURPOSE

The purpose of REVEALED is to provide true testimonies regarding racist experiences. It is my goal that this book becomes a tool that can be utilized to:

- Share our racist stories/experiences to people who find it difficult to imagine what we've gone through

- Help heal those who have chosen to reveal their impactful memories

- Spark dialogue amongst those who have yet to address their suppressed stories

We want this book to promote an exchange of dialogue in homes, churches, jobs, families, book clubs, and/or inner circles. I envision families sitting around the kitchen table discussing which stories they can relate to most while neighbors or friends begin reviewing scenarios assessing whether they may have consciously or subconsciously contributed to some of these testimonials. I'm hoping this book sparks out of the box thinking while prompting all of us to forgive, have compassion, and take the next important and courageous step to have an exchange of dialogue regarding the racist experience. I hope it results in pushing the envelope even more, picking up the phone, sending a text message or email, and asking the other person on the line if they would be willing to speak with you about this sensitive subject.

Not only will you read the true testimonies of racial experiences but you will also see how the individuals tried to learn from the opportunity and what suggestions they made in order to help history from repeating itself. I humbly ask that you practice the Willis A^3 Model (acknowledge, accept, and apologize)! It really does work as it is difficult for someone to argue after consistent and sincere apologies.

Each survey participant provided us with his or her name and title/area of expertise but we made the decision to not publish their personal information.

THE CHARGE

It was around 2:30 a.m. in the morning and all of a sudden, I heard God talking to me! The voice was very clear and said, "I want you to write a book!" I thought, oh, the charge is to write an updated version of the book I co-wrote some years ago. God nudged me again and said, "No, I want you to write about what is happening in our country and beyond." I sat up in the bed trying to deal with a hot flash at the same time saying, "Yes, I hear you God and I promise to work on it, but I will need your assistance!"

Not only did God show up, but he showed out! Literally every detail was provided and the process began on June 6, 2020. I sent a text message to family and close friends and immediately folks started responding. I knew that it needed to move fast so I started talking to others. Two of my cousins, Len and David, provided several resources and enormous encouragement, which helped confirm God's message.

So, the journey began... I then used my phone and sent my invite to everyone in my cell phone, and posted it on my personal page along with the College Bound Program's Facebook page. The next thing I knew, we had received hundreds of responses, and folks had not just one story but they had two, three, four stories speaking their truth.

As I write this introduction, I am still receiving messages from folks saying they are ready to complete the fillable form that I was able to create, thanks to my college-bound friend Angelique who walked me through the process.

Seeking the responses was the easiest part of this process. Speaking to old friends and family was the best part. Having an opportunity to catch up with people that I don't necessarily speak to everyday was awesome! It was truly a reality check for me as I began reading the testimonies that poured in. I cried while reading some and laughed at others, while being triggered for the countless racist experiences I have had to endure through my own life. Throughout the readings, I began asking myself why God had chosen me to put together these stories, because what I thought would be an easy task, turned out to be a deep process that triggered my emotions and revealed my own challenges with a variety of racist experiences. Some were common microaggressions that people of color experience almost daily; others were blatant racist indignities. In addition to my own feelings, many people I spoke with had challenges with the task as well. Some admitted that they didn't want to open up their "Pandora's box" because it hurt too much. Others admitted that they couldn't recall any racist experiences initially, but they eventually called back and said the exercise encouraged them to reflect and remember.

It is time for all of us to continue telling our stories. As I started sharing and writing down my own testimonies, I began to feel some healing and a sense of relief from getting the painful stories or memories out to the public. I actually felt a burden lifted during this process and I encourage you to take the same leap of faith. After all, we cannot control others but we can control what impacts our psyche and it is my opinion that harboring these painful stories adds to the "baggage" we carry into our relationships on the job, in the schools, and everywhere we become engaged.

We must remember that police brutality by racist cops is not the only system where racism exists. It exists in education, healthcare, retail… you name it! It is real and it is painful. COVID-19 is real and causes us to appreciate life as we learn of some folks dying while others are quarantined. The "zoomer" generation is making it very clear that the future will be different. This includes my niece Sharon Darlene, who leads the Black Lives Matter (BLM) Program in Manteca! That means that we are all required to do better… no, we MUST do better!

The testimonies have been disaggregated into a variety of categories. Some are similar, yet unique to the individual self-reporting. We ask that you not cast judgment but use this as an opportunity to self-reflect, show compassion, answer the reflection questions, be honest and candid with yourself, and then begin to have a healthy exchange of dialogue. Remember, it is okay to put the Willis A^3 Model into effect (acknowledge, accept and apologize)! Even if we feel were not wrong, it hurts us that our family, friend or foe is hurting.

I recommend you use a personal journal to list out the testimonies that you can relate to and write down the answers to the questions listed throughout the microaggression and blatant categories. Utilize a pencil instead of a pen so you can have the flexibility to write, erase, and/or re-write, truly reflecting on what you remember. In my experience, I have learned that there are always two sides to a story… there's your side and their side.

Somewhere in the middle lies the truth! It is my view that the best way to find the truth is to have an exchange of dialogue with the person and remember that everyone's perception is their reality and recognize that we cannot tell people how to feel! No one should have to defend or debate their experiences!

I thank you for taking the time to engage yourself in such a sensitive topic. Know that not only will you benefit from this read but also you will be contributing to two great causes. I am committed to donating a portion of the funds from the sale of this book to two non-profits that are near and dear to my heart–Concerned Parents Alliance/College Bound Programs and the Change4Shawn Foundation. Both are making a difference in our communities and serve as model non-profits that are committed to changing the outcome for the future when it comes to education and healthcare! You can learn more about them at www.collegeboundprograms and www.change4shawn.com.

Finally, I challenge you to ride this journey with us as we adhere to our family motto and old adage, "Once a task has begun, NEVER leave it 'til it's done; be the labor great or small, TOGETHER, we'll do it well or NOT AT ALL!!!" Now, let's REVEAL!!!

DISCLAIMERS

Author Disclaimer:

All participants volunteered to be a part of the **Revealed** book and granted permission for us to select applicable comments, experiences, and/or testimonials to be published. All submissions were voluntary with raw and first-hand testimonials from the participants.

This publication is designed to provide accurate and life tested experiences in regard to the subject matter covered. It is sold with the understanding that the author is not engaged in rendering legal, counseling, or other professional service.

Speaking or reading about racial incidents or experiences could trigger both positive and/or negative memories. Whatever memories are triggered, we encourage you to talk about it with others and seek an immediate resolution and/or assistance at your own expense. Feel free to provide us feedback about your **Revealed** experience by emailing drwillis63@gmail.com.

Publisher Disclaimer:

MEWE (Publisher) does not assume any responsibility for the accuracy, completeness, or topicality of the information provided. The statements and opinions contained in this publication are solely those of the author and individuals who provided submissions to the author for the publication and do not necessarily reflect those of the Publisher. The publisher assumes no responsibility for errors, inaccuracies, omissions, or any other inconsistencies herein and hereby disclaim any liability to any party for any loss, damage, or disruption caused by errors or omissions, whether such errors or omissions result from negligence, accident, or any other cause.

MICRO-AGGRESSION

MICRO-AGGRESSION (MA) OR COVERT DECLARATIONS

mī-krō-ə-ˈgre-shən
"A statement, action, or incident regarded as an instance of indirect, subtle, or unintentional discrimination against members of a marginalized group such as a racial or ethnic minority."
Merriam Webster Dictionary

Senior Lifestyle Reporter from Metro News, Natalie Morris says, "On their own, microaggressions may not seem like much, and they can be easy to brush off in isolation – but the accumulative effect of brushing off multiple microaggressions, every day, can be draining, demoralizing, and utterly disheartening."

A 2018 study in the *Journal of Multicultural Counseling and Development* found that of counselors who had clients reporting race-based trauma, 89% identified 'covert acts of racism' as a contributing factor.

During my research, it became evident that some people mislabel microaggressions as blatant racist experiences while others discount the seriousness of microaggressions.

Bi-Racial

MA Declaration #1

Growing up [multi-racial], I was faced with society making me choose one side or the other. For example, when filling out papers. When it came to checking the box for what race I am, most of the time it said to choose only one. That was one experience I had growing up and having to feel like I had to choose Black or Mexican. So, I would check the 'other' box. Now I am starting to notice the language changing to "check all that apply."

MA Declaration #2

I can say growing up in a pretty liberal White world, and being half-white, a majority of the racism I've faced has been that of microaggression.

In my early years, I attended a private Christian school, where I was constantly teased by my White peers for my cultural expression. As the only Black girl in my class, my hairstyles would often cause alarm and snickers from young girls who believed their look was superior to mine. At only seven years old, I would come home crying to my mother about how I wanted to have White people's hair and look more White. Upon reflection, it was because I felt unloved for who I was.

Public school wasn't much better. The parents of my White friends often automatically assumed I must be the negative influence when their children were having difficulties in behavior or school. I wasn't a bad kid either. I was very studious and smart, but when I would participate in reckless behavior with friends, I was always put in the position of being the delinquent, whereas their wrong doings were only viewed as mistakes.

In high school came deeper connections with other Black people because the population was much larger. The only difference was that I didn't talk the same, and I liked a lot of things considered weird. I found a lot of my experiences growing up to feel like I didn't belong anywhere. At the time, I was too young to understand the racism rooted in the cultural norms; for instance, when I would get [tan] in the summer, my friends would make comments that I was too dark as a joke. We had all been fed the same narratives growing up. The domino effect made me want to embrace the norms established from colonization like wearing weaves and damaging my hair with heat to be more appealing, instead of embracing my true natural self and new ideas of beauty, which I still am having to work to reprogram to this day.

Being that I am [multi-racial], I have witnessed microaggressions against people who are darker than I am, which to me is still a direct insult to Black people as a whole. Being told things like "you're pretty for a black girl," "I want a mixed baby like you," or "you're so exotic" serves to devalue my blackness and suggest that if I was 100% Black I wouldn't be as valuable. The list goes on.

MA Declaration #3

My daughter is mixed-race and was born in Zimbabwe. Her father is a Black Zimbabwean. My ex-husband and I moved to the states when she turned two years old and decided to live in my hometown of Manteca, California. Although Manteca has a more diverse population now, this has not always been the case. It seemed that every time I went to the store with my daughter, people always said something similar: "She's so beautiful! Is she adopted?" I found this offensive on two fronts. The assumption that she must be adopted because she is a different race implied that it was not acceptable for a White woman to have a child with a Black man. Secondly, the statement also implied that any child of color must be in need of adoption due to their difficult circumstances. The fact is that my daughter is beautiful, born of two people who love each other very much, and who just happen to be different races. This is certainly not something that should have to ever be explained to complete strangers.

MA Declaration #4

I have many examples [of microaggressions]. A few include the following: Assuming my parents are not Black or that I am bi-racial because my parents are not dark. Assuming that I am a good dancer, singer, athlete, grew up poor, or like certain foods. Consistently calling me "not really black" because I do not fit a certain stereotype that the individual has in their head. As a kid, having to play Jackie Robinson or Martin Luther King at school events. Being followed around in stores. Talking to someone on the phone and then, when meeting them in person, them saying, "That is not what I thought you looked like."

Black Slang

MA Declaration #1
On occasion, I have been told by my White associates that I was "jiving" or asked what my angle was.

MA Declaration #2
I'm the only Black person at my job and my White counterparts always come up to me trying to speak like a Black person using slang. They hold out their hand saying, "What's up my brotha?"

But You're Different

MA Declaration #1
Being told I am a different type of Black person. I speak so well, or I must be an athlete. All while co-workers only reference Black movies around me.

MA Declaration #2
Being told, "You are different from *them*."

MA Declaration #3
"You're kidding right? You're not really Black! Hey guys, did you know so and so was Black?"

Certain Assignments

MA Declaration #1
Professional administrative appointments were based on the ethnic makeup of the school. I was told by the county superintendent to stay out of school districts where I didn't belong, like Poway and East County

schools. As a special education teacher, I was relegated to classes and neighborhood schools that were predominantly Black or minority.

MA Declaration #2
Being told, "You may want to stay in the multi-cultural field because Black people tend to get those jobs."

MA Declaration #3
"Are you sure you want to be a Scientist? This is an area that not many Blacks are getting into."

Dining

MA Declaration #1
African Americans experience constant subtle discrimination to the point where you think, "Was that what I thought it was?" My most recent experience happened today while waiting in line to place my food order and a Caucasian man just walked right in front of me and started to place his food order.

MA Declaration #2
When I was out of town at a nice restaurant in Monterey with my wife, an elderly White man was loudly talking, saying "People don't know how to behave in nice restaurants!" He then went on to reiterate everything we ordered and was complaining that our wine did not go with the food we ordered.

MA Declaration #3
In the early 1970s, I went to dinner with two friends who were White. We went to Carrows Restaurant in Colton, CA. It was "seat yourself," so we sat in a booth and waited. There was only one other booth occupied in the place. We called over a waitress and were ignored.

One of the people I was with then went and talked to the waitress and she indicated she was coming. After about 10 minutes, we asked to speak to the manager who never came over. After another 5 minutes, we left. Just shows that even in the early 1970s in California, racism and Jim Crow was still in existence and very prevalent.

MA Declaration #4
"Oh, that sign should have been turned around, we're closed!"

Education

MA Declaration #1
As early as 10 years old, I became a "pen-pal" from the list of names within our Christian Sunday School lesson book with another child. We wrote letters to each other for months. We talked about activities within our churches, school, our homes, and family. She was from Mendenhall, Mississippi. After I told her I was Black, she never wrote me back.

MA Declaration #2
In the 1970s, I was bused to a junior high and high school in very wealthy areas of West Los Angeles–Paul Revere Jr. High in Brentwood, CA, and Palisades High School in the Pacific Palisades. At Paul Revere, in American History class we had to research historical figures. We had a list to select from; there was not one African American on the list. There were only two African Americans in the class–myself and another girl. Her mom was a teacher. Her mom made sure we selected African American historical figures. My friend wrote about Harriet Tubman, and I selected Frederick Douglas.

MA Declaration #3
During high school, we had school spirit days where we could dress up to represent different decades. We had a 50's dress-up day where all the students wore attire reminiscent of the 1950s (Bobby socks, Poodle Skirts, etc.). I dressed up too and one White male student came up to me and said,

"Why did you dress up? There were no Blacks in the 1950s; you all came out in the 1960s." It really hurt my feelings. He was my friend, and was laughing when he said it.

MA Declaration #4
My White supervisor asked me whether there was a difference between using the term "nigger" as opposed to the term "nigga."

MA Declaration #5
One example that comes to mind occurred during my junior year of high school. As a class, we were discussing some of the racial topics in the book, *The Adventures of Huckleberry Finn*. We covered the history of how most African Americans used to only be able to find work in the motor industry. As we were closing up the conversation, in front of my class, my former teacher asked me if my parents worked in the motor industry.

MA Declaration #6
My high school counselor (Galileo HS in San Francisco, CA) was trying to discourage me from going to a 4-year college. I was an "A" student but the Junior College course is what she wanted to put me on. I went to HBCU, Tougaloo College–best decision I ever made!

MA Declaration #7
In my 9th grade History class, every question about Africa was directed towards me first, as if I was supposed to already know specific things about the different countries.

MA Declaration #8
Professors offered me a position to organize their research materials but offered male classmates actual research positions. I often get the "you don't look like an engineer." If they learn I emigrated from Mexico, "you speak very good English."

MA Declaration #9
People are often surprised that I have a PhD, no matter where I have worked.

MA Declaration #10
I remember an incident in the 5th or 6th grade during the era of busing. I attended a school where most of the Black children were bused in as a part of integration efforts but I actually lived in the neighborhood. I did something that warranted detention and the yard supervisor remarked that I could not be given after school detention because I was a busing student. I immediately corrected her, informing her that I lived near the school. I walked to school and did not take the bus. My remarks must have taken the yard supervisor by surprise and she had me go to the office.

Once in the office, I was questioned by the school secretary whose address was my mother using and again, I repeated that was my home address. Again, I was not believed. I remember feeling like I was being interrogated. The secretary decided that she was done with me and called my mother at work. I knew my mother had an important meeting that day and I advised the school secretary that today would not be a good day to call my mother at work over something that was not an emergency (all Black children know the "don't call my Mama at work unless it is an emergency" rule). Long story short, once my mother got on the phone, that school secretary probably thought my mother was going to come through the phone as my mother proceeded to let the school know that we lived at the address on file and not to dare question our residence again.

MA Declaration #11
Being told that you're "smart for a Black guy," or even being told by your HS counselor that you'll be fine getting into college because you're Black.

MA Declaration #12
In college, we had to write a paper of a significant event in our lives. Another Black student asked the question of what if there wasn't anything that would be considered particularly significant to write about. The instructor told the student that he fully believed that she had no significance in her life.

MA Declaration #13

Providing art supplies where beige is the only "skin color."

MA Declaration #14

Over-diagnosing Black students with learning disabilities.

MA Declaration #15

Acting more patient and understanding to White and light-skinned students…

MA Declaration #16

Punishing Black students at a higher rate than their non-Black peers for doing the same thing.

MA Declaration #17

Only interacting with Black parents/guardians when their child is a "serious problem!"

MA Declaration #18

Teaching students to "ignore each other's differences" …they call this color blindness!

MA Declaration #19

Discounting our Black kids when they report that they've traveled to another country over the summertime.

MA Declaration #20

Informing Black students that they are going to "wind up in jail" or that they will "never make it out of the hood!"

MA Declaration #21

Telling Black scholars that they will "NEVER amount to anything" and demanding they take trade courses instead of A-G!

MA Declaration #22
When a Black student gets in trouble, calling the police immediately instead of talking with the student to see if the allegations are true!

MA Declaration #23
Being told by a teacher, "Your hair is cute but it's a major distraction!"

MA Declaration #24
Being in the teacher break room and hearing other teachers talk bad about the Black kids!

MA Declaration #25
Always blaming the Black kids when they hear noises and making them go to the office.

MA Declaration #26
During my senior year of high school, I was accepted into a competitive university. Many of my peers also applied to the university; however, they were denied admission. Despite my hard work in and outside of school, my peers assumed that I was only admitted into the university as a result of Affirmative Action. My peers did not care about their grades nearly as much as I did and focused more on the social aspect of school. I was admitted into the university as a result of my hard work and perseverance and my peers tried to take that away from me.

MA Declaration #27
There were only two Blacks in my graduate program and we were both females. They called her my name and me her name. On several occasions, they handed me her graded paper and vice versa.

MA Declaration #28
While being the only two Black students in our cohort, we were often seen as the spokespersons for the Black community. Every time a question

came about regarding something related to the Black community, all heads turned to us so we could answer.

MA Declaration #29

I have experienced microaggressions my entire life. There was a time when I thought that the more educated and successful, by society's standard, I became, [the more] things would change. Still, I encounter microaggressions, even now, as one of the most senior executive leaders of my organization.

Having three master's degrees, two doctorate degrees, and even a post-doc hasn't changed that. I am a Black woman, and thriving through, educating through, and often with welling eyes, pressing through microaggressions, has become my normal.

One example of a microaggression that I experience quite often is people not believing that I am the boss, and once learning that it's true, preferring to speak to someone else. One day, a visitor came to my office. The Secretary asked them to wait for me in the lobby. When I came out, they expressed that they wanted to speak to the Director. I identified myself by name and as the Director. They requested then to speak to who's in charge. Just as I was about to explain that I am the person they needed to meet with, one of my White male subordinate colleagues walked by.

He advised them that they needed to speak with me and identified himself as support staff. Then he looked toward me and said, "The doctor is here!" One of the visitors responded, "Oh, you're the doctor?" Blinded by my Blackness, they'd not even heard my name. Bruised hearted, I smiled, shook their hands, invited them into my office, and tended to their needs with genuine care.

I did attempt to engage them in inquiry and asked why they didn't want to meet with me before. Never answering my question, they all just smiled and complimented me on the plaques that were hanging on the wall and told me that I should be proud of myself. This specific incident was seven years ago; I remember it as if it were yesterday.

Entertainment

MA Declaration #1
A White colleague stated that I probably got hired/cast in operas because I'm Black.

MA Declaration #2
I was the only Black cast member and every time they talked about a Black topic, everyone looked my way.

MA Declaration #3
"Wow, I am not surprised you can sing because Black people have such great voices."

MA Declaration #4
"I knew it, I knew it! Black people really have soul!"

Hair and Beauty

MA Declaration #1
I first decided to go natural working for two White male attorneys. I wore my hair in a wash and go, which shrank up to a complete Afro by the time I got to work. The older attorney said he liked my hair and that it reminded him of the Black Panther movement. I was honestly thrown back so I just smiled.

MA Declaration #2
I am a member of a group of Moms who meet once a month for happy hour and/or a movie. There are six of us. Four are White, one is Latina, and me. Every time I get a haircut (I recently went natural), one of them makes a big deal out of wanting to touch my hair. As far as I know, she has never said this to any of the others. It's not a huge thing, but I find it demeaning and disrespectful.

MA Declaration #3
I was on the BART platform at EC Plaza when a White woman came to me and complimented me on my hair (it was in a natural fro) and then she proceeded to ask me whether I had on a wig.

MA Declaration #4
Being asked if someone can touch my hair, asking how I get my hair cut, or being asked if someone can pick my hair.

MA Declaration #5
Being told to stand behind the counsel chairs and "wait for my lawyer." I was in a suit with a briefcase, but my hair was in braids. I had to prove I was a lawyer and show my bar card.

MA Declaration #6
While pressing my hair in my dorm suite bathroom, girls took turns coming in and out asking, "Does that hurt?" They let the entire suite know that the "burning smell" was from the Black girl combing her hair with a hot comb!

HBCU

MA Declaration #1
I attended an HBCU (Historically Black College or University) for my undergraduate studies. During a job interview with an older White male, I was asked whether or not my school, Morgan State University, was an accredited college/university.

MA Declaration #2
My leadership skills and decisions are constantly questioned by White and Hispanic colleagues in my department. They minimize my HBCU institution, experience, and mentor professors, but also say I'm "different from others" because my graduate studies were at an SEC (University of Mississippi).

14

MA Declaration #3
We've changed the language from PWI (Predominantly White Institutions) to HWI (Historically White Institutions).

Healthcare

MA Declaration #1
Once, on a nurse travel assignment, I was given a camp cot to sleep on after working 12-hour shifts in a hospital in Texas. I was also not given a key to the apartment that I was sharing with my White roommate. She, on the other hand, had a double bed with full linen and ruffles, in addition to a key to the front door. My key was to the back door that was off the alley and a dark staircase.

MA Declaration #2
Having a physician tell me, "Wow, I'm really jealous of you Black people as your skin is so beautiful!"

MA Declaration #3
"No, you're not really 55?! Black people really age well!"

Housing/Residential

MA Declaration #1
I signed a teaching contract for a Detroit suburb during my senior year at the University of Michigan. When my parents and I found an available apartment in that suburb, we visited the complex only to be told, "Oh, sorry, that unit is no longer available."

MA Declaration #2
Just one of the experiences I have had was very recent. Moving from California to Nevada, I planned on starting a new life with new

experiences, but it was the worst decision I made. The apartment I moved into was called "Cyan" and was located in Henderson. From day one of moving in, the leasing office staff coerced me into paying more money than what I was told. They told me $300, but when I arrived, with the moving truck outside, the lady wouldn't give me the key unless I paid a full month's rent ($1200). While I had no choice but to empty out my bank account, I complied.

So, I asked them, "Since I have to pay all this extra money, can I park in the parking space directly in front of my door, that belonged to absolutely no one?" The maintenance guy said yes. Two weeks later, I started receiving ORANGE stickers on my window. Every day, I went into that office twice. The first time I was very relaxed and calm and I told them that they already agreed to me parking there.

Two weeks later, and eleven ORANGE stickers later, I proceeded to the office a SECOND time. Somewhat agitated and miserable that my new place in a new state is going this badly, I said to them in a low but aggressive voice, "This needs to stop now." Me being a 6 foot 2 Black man, with a voice similar to Barry White's, the White lady waited for me to leave and then proceeded to lock the leasing office, and then locked herself in her back office. I left and went back to my apartment, in the back of the apartment [complex]. I thought nothing of it.

Approximately ten minutes later, I had two White Henderson police officers knocking at my door. As I'm talking to them from my upstairs balcony, they threatened to get an arrest warrant if I didn't come down to talk to them. So, I agreed to go down there with one demand of not going to jail. They agreed. I got down there and we were talking, while my girlfriend was recording. After 20 minutes of talk, the very last thing one of the cops said to me was, "The girl felt scared of you and for that, I need you to put your hands behind your back, before I use force."

After telling him, "You played me," I complied. I went to jail for five days, charged with harassment, got probation for a year, and had to pay a fine. I get out of jail with an eviction notice on my door telling me to vacate the property within the next 24hrs. I never had an eviction in my entire LIFE, until I got to Henderson, NV.

MA Declaration #3

In 1969, we looked at a house in San Leandro, CA. A church was selling the house. The neighborhood did not want Blacks in the house. The minister said not to worry, and he would walk with me and the girls to school every day to keep us safe. I told my husband that we were not interested in being pioneers, plus he worked nights, so we declined.

MA Declaration #4

Being a person of color in a predominantly White neighborhood.

MA Declaration #5

Someone coming to my door asking me if the homeowner was home.

MA Declaration #6

Moved into an all-white neighborhood and was constantly picked on.

MA Declaration #7

I was 4 years old and my parents purchased a home in a community called Skyline where there was only one White family left on our street. I recall asking my mother how did all these Black people end up in the same area and at that time I did not know anything about redlining. Looking back, I realized that this was not the first time. When my parents first came to San Diego, they lived on B Street, which is now known as a part of downtown San Diego. From there, they moved to Encina Drive which is located near Lincoln High School and then to Skyline. What frustrated me most was watching someone coming to our home to do a refinance and wondering why my parents could not go to a bank. What saddens me is after 43 years of institutional racism, my father died only to lose their home from a faulty reverse mortgage. As a result of this experience, I vowed that no financial institution would dictate where I could live.

MA Declaration #8

"I've watched your family for some time and wanted you to know that we really like Black people. I just wanted you to know."

MA Declaration #9
When we were moving from Northern CA to Southern CA, all my White colleagues insisted that we should move to Oceanside because that's where we could find more people that looked like us.

MA Declaration #10
It was as if everyone knew when the only Black family in the development was going on a daily walk in the neighborhood. As we walked around, it seemed like they all came out to watch us. They didn't speak but they stared at us until we moved past their house.

MA Declaration #11
When the White people in the neighborhood walked by our house and our garage was up, they stopped and it appeared to us that they were wondering how we could have a BMW and Mercedes in the garage.

MA Declaration #12
Being one of few Black families in our neighborhood, we had to purchase a camera system because our lawn had become the "poop" place for all the neighborhood dogs.

MA Declaration #13
My husband and I were having difficulty finding this specific restaurant we were looking for. We found ourselves in a nearby residential area. There was a man doing yard work. He was White. He saw us approaching as we drove down the street. When we reached his house, I lowered my window and asked, "Excuse me, can you please give us directions?" When he didn't respond, I asked again a little louder this time. Still no response. But this time he got up and went into his garage, ignoring us altogether.

MA Declaration #14
I responded to an ad where an apartment opening was available but when I got there in person, they told me it was no longer available.

Judgment

MA Declaration #1

When I am in meetings, many people are surprised to see me and to know that I am the expert in the room. They ask me about my credentials and how long it takes to become a Diagnostician.

MA Declaration #2

I was raised in a working class, Irish Catholic neighborhood in Boston in the 1950s-60s. Rich, educated Protestants are still, to this day called "Brahmins" in Boston. I was at a college mixer, dancing with a young man who asked me where I went to school. My answer gave him the "clues" to my identity. He then told me, "I could never date you. My parents would kill me. You're poor and you're Catholic."

MA Declaration #3

On occasions too numerous to count, I have experienced microaggression from White people. One of the most common and ongoing occurs when I am in public and White women clutch their purse when seeing me.

MA Declaration #4

Being an African American male, this is a common experience for me. To connect the most essential concerns I must address the psychological dismantling of the African American male. It happens all the time, but I took note in junior high school. We had to walk a few miles to our junior high school (Ponce De Leon Jr. High), located in Coral Gables, Florida. I had to cross major highways on route to the school. As a group of us would cross in the crossway at the light, we would hear doors locking as if we were thugs who were going to attack people in their cars. We were seventh and eighth graders just walking to school. It really bothered me why people would do that, treating us like common criminals while prejudging our character.

MA Declaration #5

I was in my second to third year of school and I had just given birth to my first child. I became a single parent during school, while being eight hours away from home. I had just returned to school and my child accompanied me to some of my classes the first semester back. With a new baby, there were several times that I had to excuse myself due my son beginning to cry. I remember one particular evening where I had to excuse myself and returned just as class was getting out. I remember gathering my things and the professor stopping me to say, "You know that you are never going to pass my class like this." That statement stung really, really bad... like it hit me to my core. I was a new mother, supporting myself, trying to get through school, trying to do my best, and I have a professor say something like this to me. Again, the Black population at this school was only about 2% with the student body being around 25,000 or so. I have never let go of that statement and it still makes me angry that he would say something like that to me. I could have used a, "How can I be of help.... Is there anything that you need by way of additional support, etc." No, it was a blanket statement that I was going to fail. I remember getting my first exam score back in that class and as he passed them out, he told me that I received the highest grade in the class for that exam. I don't know if that was his way of apologizing to me... I will never know.

MA Declaration #6

As an African American male, living in the midst of these current chaotic and historic times, microaggression has noticeably skyrocketed. Although I have not yet had a first-hand opportunity to experience this on a verbal level, I have in fact had several encounters with numerous individuals who show a strong bias towards my ethnicity. Whether it be choosing to take another elevator, clutching a purse tighter, and even avoiding eye contact or staring at me in public. These are just a FEW of the behavioral prejudices that I have experienced as a young Black man in America.

MA Declaration #7

For quite some time now, there has been an established perception of African Americans and Blacks being labeled as rowdy, ghetto, poor individuals "who have nothing to lose." To the extent that Donald J. Trump, the President of the United States, has shared similar messages with the media and even demonstrated a lack of empathy, let alone an understanding of these recent events. Not once have we disregarded the mistakes and unacceptable behavior demonstrated by our own people, but to simply ignore the obvious and blatant exposure of a bigger issue is essentially justifying it. This is why Black and Brown people still experience microaggressions, myself included.

MA Declaration #8
Two ladies approached me to ask what race I was because l looked mixed and not all Black. I told them and one said, "But you're beautiful." So, I can't be all Black and beautiful?

MA Declaration #9
I had a Korean manager who would call on me to repeat certain words because my southern accent could be heard. She wanted to embarrass me.

MA Declaration #10
When I was 18 years old, I moved to SoCal to attend college. I went out with a new friend from my dorm and we went to a party. At the party, my friend and I were the only people of color. It seemed like everyone was staring at us when we walked into the party. We saw a friendly face, someone we both knew from class and started talking to them and their friends. One of the girls in the group asked me randomly "what I was." She wanted to know my race. I told her I was mixed, Black and Mexican. She started laughing and everyone in the group laughed. The girl thought I was joking. She soon realized I was not laughing. She said "You're Black? Seriously?" The rest of the night, she purposely did not acknowledge my presence and only talked to others in the group.

MA Declaration #11
When I tell non-Blacks that I am from Los Angeles, it is assumed that I am straight out of Compton or Watts, CA.

MA Declaration #12
When I was in the eighth grade, I had a Puerto Rican teacher who identified as White. I liked this teacher. One day she asked me if I was half-white and I told her no, but back in history I have a little White blood. She told me "Oh, that's why you're pretty." I didn't know what to say. All

I could do was kind of smile. As I got older, I realized that I don't have to be half-white to be beautiful, because Black is beautiful.

MA Declaration #13
After a snowboarding trip, my friend's uncle purchased a variety of drinks for everyone. As he was passing them out, he let us know that the grape soda was specifically for me. I laughed it off to avoid making the situation awkward for the remainder of the trip.

MA Declaration #14
Being told I look like a thug because I was wearing a Du-rag.

MA Declaration #15
"You sound angry when you talk."

MA Declaration #16
"You have a very aggressive personality."

MA Declaration #17
"We are all leaders, so not getting a promotion shouldn't bother you."

MA Declaration #18
You would be surprised what people say about your hair.

MA Declaration #19
You continue to scream at people... I just have a loud voice coming from a large family.

MA Declaration #20
Unfortunately, my first encounter with racism was within my own family. My maternal grandparents were from West Virginia and they were an interracial couple. My maternal grandmother had limited

education. Her primary responsibility was as homemaker. My maternal grandfather also had limited education and worked in the coal mines. My maternal grandparents moved to Ohio and lived there their entire married life, as far as I remember. My family would occasionally take vacations to West Virginia because my maternal grandparents still had family living there. The first time I met my great-grandmother she referred to me as the dark one. I guess compared to her White skin I would be dark to her. I was about six or seven years of age and was deeply hurt. My father has a dark complexion and my mother's complexion is fair. I never thought about my complexion until my great-grandmother pointed it out to me.

MA Declaration # 21
Just today, a mechanic refused to work on my car with the excuse that he didn't want the liability. He stated that my car was "not safe" to drive, but refused to do anything to help me fix the problem. Why? He judged that I didn't "have the money" to fix the problem based on my appearance.

MA Declaration # 22
I've been told that Black people are curses descended from the people of Hann.

MA Declaration #23
Being stopped by the police and asked, "Is this your car?" My car is a black convertible Mercedes.

MA Declaration #24
I have heard it all, even from White in-laws in my own family! During our first meeting, I overheard my soon-to-be White father in law say to my White fiancé, "You got yourself an expensive piece of black ass there Sonny!" He was referring to the way I was dressed and my car.

MA Declaration #25
We moved to Antioch, CA, in 1979. I remember going to the store with my mom at nine years old. The salesperson asked my mom to verify her

address and before my mom could say the city, they would say Pittsburg. My mom would say, "No, I live in Antioch," and they'd give her "a look."

MA Declaration #26
"ALL lives matter!"

Law/Judicial

MA Declaration #1
In my Criminal Law class, we had a case about a Chinese woman shooting and killing a little Black girl over some orange juice that she thought the little girl stole, when in actuality she had put the money on the counter. The professor kept trying to justify the Chinese woman's "fear" despite the fact that the little girl had her back towards the woman when she was shot and killed. The professor said the little Black girl was the aggressor and it was self-defense. I was so upset that I had to go up to the professor after class and ask why she said the little girl was the aggressor. She said it was because she pushed the woman first. I then politely asked didn't the woman grab her backpack, and isn't that assault according to our torts class, so wasn't the woman the aggressor? She asked me if I was sure the woman did that. I was 100% sure, so I said yes I was. Her only response was that she wasn't aware and needed to go back and read the case.

MA Declaration #2
After years of law school and passing the bar, I finally get my first case and as soon as I go to the attorney area, I am stopped by a bailiff saying, "Excuse me, this area is for attorneys only!"

MA Declaration #3
"You're actually a judge? No way!"

MA Declaration #4
Hearing whispers in the hallway and people saying, "There's a Black judge in this chamber! You should check him out!"

24

Looking Suspicious

MA Declaration #1
I have been followed around the store.

MA Declaration #2
I had my own Teaching Assistant (TA) call the police on me because he "thought I looked suspicious."

MA Declaration #3
I have seen women clinch their purses when I enter the elevator.

MA Declaration #4
When driving for delivery services, I have been asked several times to show proof on my phone that I am there to pick up a delivery. People look outside of the peephole and ask that I leave the food on the ground rather than open the door and interact with a Black male.

MA Declaration #5
Just this past weekend, while walking in my own neighborhood in Orange County, CA (I have lived here 28 years), I was doing laps around the parking lot of the junior high about a mile from my home. I used to walk around the school's oval track, but due to the pandemic and school being closed, I now just walk laps around the parking lot. Just as I was entering the lot to begin my first lap, a Cypress police cruiser pulled into the lot behind me, slowly passed me up, and then stopped several yards in front of me. I was on the phone with a friend, and I asked her to stay on the phone with me, as I was afraid of a confrontation with the police for "walking while Black" and wanted her to at least be an "ear" witness if I was approached. I passed his car and kept walking, and did my laps while he sat there in the car.

Trying to rationalize the situation in my own head, I began to wonder if there had been a break-in at the school or if he was just eating his breakfast, but I was actually afraid and wasn't about to approach the police car to ask, even though I knew I had done nothing wrong. When I exited the parking lot to head home, at that point the police car pulled off. I still don't know why they were there. I told my (non-Black) neighbor later that day about it, and she immediately said that I should have gone up and asked what's going on. I told her that she did not understand the fear I lived with as a Black person and mother of a Black son (who jogs at dusk every day in our neighborhood just like Ahmaud Arbery), and that walking up to the police could be seen as an act of provocation that I may not live through.

Military

MA Declaration #1
I recall, while attending Coast Guard Officer Candidate School in the mid 1990s, where I was the only Black male in my class. One of my White instructors would often make a point to single me out for minor issues while in training. The situation eventually escalated to a point where he fabricated a negative performance report, which could have resulted in my removal from the training program.

MA Declaration #2
Being the only Black officer, my name was often forgotten by my commanders.

Movie Theater

MA Declaration #1
I have an older sister, brother, and younger sister. My family moved to Compton from Texas in 1955-56. At the time, Negroes did not live past the double yellow on Wilmington Avenue. My eldest sister is the darkest one of the children, and the rest of us are very fair. One day she took us to the movies in downtown Compton and she asked the ticket lady for three tickets. The lady asked my sister who the other two tickets were for. My sister replied, "For my brother and sister." The White woman looked bug-eyed at us like she was going to fall through the glass in the ticket booth.

MA Declaration #2
When I was in high school, I had a job at our local movie theater. Early in my job there, I was working concessions and an older White man came to

26

purchase a tub of popcorn. I gave my usual dialog of, "Would you like a large, and would you like butter with that?" He looked at me oddly and said, "You speak English really well, why is that?" I responded, "I'm in AP English, so I would expect so." After my response, he asked, "Where are you from?" I responded, "Around here." He followed with, "No really, where are you from?" I responded, "I was born in Pittsburgh, PA." At this point, I was super irritated, but he was still a customer and I was fairly new at my job. I gave him the popcorn and rang up the total. I told him how much he owed. After taking his money, he finished with, "I wanted to know where you really were from."

My Neighbor Is Black

MA Declaration #1
I have had work colleagues make the comment, "I have a Black or Hispanic friend," or words to that effect. I consider this unintentional racism because I don't think you should need to qualify the ethnic background of a friend, if they are a friend. The comment is usually made because the person is uncomfortable with the story being told and knows that there is a hint of racism being demonstrated.

MA Declaration #2
I'm always leery when someone that is non-Black starts off a conversation by saying, "My neighbors are Black" so I can identify. I automatically stop listening! Why do they do that?

MA Declaration #3
"You remind me of my neighbor… she's Black."

Non-Black

MA Declaration #1
My first memory of racism comes from the viewpoint of a seven-year-old little girl. We were a typical middle-class family. My parents were friends

with a Black family, Mr. and Mrs. Levi. They had two daughters around my age. On one visit in the summer of 1964, the Levi's asked my parents if I could go to Disneyland with them. Disneyland! I was so excited. My parents said no. I was devastated. I threw a fit. I overheard my folks discussing letting me go but that I couldn't because I was White and they were Black. From a seven-year-old point of view, this made no sense. How unfair... only Black people could go to Disneyland! I told my parents they were lucky and I wished I was Black. I don't remember their response. Years later, I talked to my parents about this incident. There had been rioting in Los Angeles and other places. My folks feared for our safety–a Black family traveling with a White little girl. They could never forgive themselves if any harm had come to me or the Levi family.

MA Declaration #2
In my personal experience as a Latina, I have experienced more microaggressions than blatant racist attacks. There are people who have tried to use my race, sex, or a combination of the two to undermine me or my intelligence. For instance, I have had coworkers and bosses question my authority when speaking on a topic I am knowledgeable about and qualified to discuss, when they would not do this with my White peers.

MA Declaration #3
I have felt out of place time and time again in mainly White professional events, jobs, and classrooms.

MA Declaration #4
I have been called out as if I was the waitress in a restaurant where I was a fellow customer.

MA Declaration #5
People ask me loudly if I speak English. In a conversation about careers, people not asking what I do for a living and then being surprised that I work. If my job comes up, asking for clarity on my position–"Are you CEO of the whole company?"

Police

MA Declaration #1
I have had officers ask if I was on parole or probation during traffic stops, along with having officers ask other people in the car if I was on parole or probation.

MA Declaration #2
Being stopped by the police and asked, "Is this your car?"

MA Declaration #3
When I was eighteen, I took music lessons from someone who lives in Bel Air. I would have my lesson every Sunday morning. I owned a 1964 Buick Riviera and without fail, the Beverly Hills PD would pull me over EVERY Sunday, and sometimes twice in one day, going to the lesson and returning home. It frustrated me to the point where I would pull over as soon as they got behind me knowing what was coming next.

MA Declaration #4
Told not to be stopped by police officers six times for being smart, or not qualified for a position before given the opportunity to perform.

MA Declaration #5
At the age of seventeen, I was threatened by police to be quiet or I'd get arrested. I was only asking the police to lower their weapons that they had drawn on our front porch after responding to a call of shots fired. About 20 cops showed up to my family's home, weapons drawn and pointed, ready to shoot first and ask questions later. About 10 of them came up to our front door. My mother answered and they disrespected her by questioning and treating her as a perpetrator instead of the victim.

So, being the young bright-eyed rebel/militant BPP/Civil rights agitator that I was in the early 1970s, I spoke up and demanded that they stop pointing their guns at my house, my mother, and my siblings. I was told to shut the f__k up or go to jail. For what? Demanding to be treated with respect and dignity! What happened next was a major explosion of events that traumatized me and my family and the whole neighborhood. I was snatched up and drug off my front porch. After a fight, dog attack, gunshot, dog killed, and my first arrest (with my brother), I was booked and charged with resisting arrest and inciting a riot because all of the neighborhood kids attacked the cops who were trying to beat me and drag me to the ground. In jail, my brother and I got into another fight with the jailer while in a holding cell. In conclusion, I'm blessed to be here today. This minor incident was turned into a life threatening moment that could have been resolved peacefully, if only my folks had been treated respectfully by the racist cops of Indianapolis in 1971.

MA Declaration #6

Coming home in the evening from a batting lesson that I was teaching, I decided to cut through the neighborhood of million dollar homes to shorten the amount of time it took to get to my home. I got pulled over by a police officer and I could not understand the reason as to why I was being pulled over. He came up to my window and asked me where I was coming from. I told him I came through the neighborhood from a batting lesson and was on my way home. He told me that he stopped me because he had a report that someone in a dark purple sedan was sitting outside of the house and it looked suspicious. I informed him that my car was red and I drove through the neighborhood and did not stop. He stated that red may look like purple at night and then proceeded to ask for my driver's license.

At the time, my wallet was underneath my seat so I asked him if I could grab it from under the seat so that I may hand it to him. He watched me intently as I grabbed my wallet and I took out my driver's license and handed it to him. He wrote down my name and driver's license number in his notepad and then returned my license to me. He instructed me that that was all he needed and let me go on my way. At the time, I could not understand why I was being stopped and after explaining it to my dad he helped me draw the conclusion that I was most likely pulled over because the police officer assumed that because of my race and where I was coming from it was suspicious as to why I would be going through that neighborhood in the first place.

MA Declaration #7

I lived in an apartment in Torrance in the 1980s. I was working for Frito Lay Inc. and going to work at 3:30 am. I was sitting on the porch waiting on my ride to work when the Torrance Police drove by, shining the light on me, and asking why I was sitting on that porch. My answer was that I lived there and was waiting on my ride to work. They turned off the light and kept going.

MA Declaration #8

Stopped by the local police for being Black.

MA Declaration #9

When I was nineteen years old, my friend and I experienced police brutality from a White police officer and a Black police officer. As we were walking at night, there was a dark Buick Regal that pulled in front of us from the opposite direction. They shouted, "Put your hands up!" We were handcuffed from behind and placed face down on the hood of a police car at 1:30 a.m. in the morning. The White police officer asked if we had any drugs on us and checked our pockets. We said, "No." He asked for our ID and then he told us to run as fast as we can. At that moment, I thought he would shoot us in the back. We made it home safely.

MA Declaration #10

There were four Black males, all dressed in suits, returning home from my cousin's mother's funeral in Inglewood, CA, and all of a sudden three police cars surrounded us. We explained the situation but they still made us get out of the car and sit, in handcuffs, on the curb. They came back about 30 minutes later and claimed that our car was reported in another crime and they wanted to make sure it wasn't us. They just returned our ID's and never even apologized.

Qualifications

MA Declaration #1

As a mid-level associate attorney at a prestigious Wall Street law firm, I was recruited by a partner to come work with him at another "white shoe" firm. I made arrangements to visit the firm and was interviewed by several attorneys, including the senior partner of the firm. The partner then took me over to meet two (White female) mid-level associate attorneys so that they could take me to lunch and tell me more about the firm. On our way out, they asked if I wanted to see what my office would look like (if I took the job). I said yes, and they took me to a small, interior, windowless office with two or three desks inside. I was surprised (all of the attorneys I knew at law firms had offices to themselves with windows), and asked them if their offices looked like this. They both looked at me in surprise, and basically said, "No, we're attorneys. This is where you'll be sitting as a paralegal." They just assumed I was a paralegal, even though I had been introduced to them by the most senior partner in their firm and was clearly being recruited. I called them on their "mistake" and knew at that instant that I would never work at that firm.

MA Declaration #2
After I received a promotion, an older White male inquired, "How did you get that job?"

MA Declaration #3
While working at UC Berkeley, in the 1990s, through the Ombudsperson Office I learned that several workplace colleagues (African Americans) were feeling discriminated against based on work assignments, comments, performance evaluations, and lack of advancement/promotional opportunities. Given the many complaints, the Department of Justice was asked to review the department's practices, policies, and procedures.

MA Declaration #4
As the only Black female in my department, a complaint was launched against me for placing "God bless" in my closing emails. They said folks complained that I was being too religious.

Retail

MA Declaration #1
Often when I go through department stores, employees/security guards will single me out and glare at me while I go about my business.

Sometimes if they are really bothered by my presence they will come by and ask, "Can I help you with something?" with the same suspicious look, while only moments later smiling and waving at White customers.

MA Declaration #2
I've been ignored in stores and overlooked in favor of a White person to be assisted.

MA Declaration #3
Being followed around department stores, to being completely ignored when I enter or leave.

MA Declaration #4
Just off the top of my head, a cashier rang me up and asked for payment. She not only assumed that I was not spending cash to purchase my items, but instructed me on how to put my EBT card into the machine. I did not have an EBT card.

MA Declaration #5
Most of my blatant racial experiences have been because the person thinks I am Asian or Spanish. I have had several microaggression situations. I went to the store and used my credit card. The clerk asked me for not one ID, but two forms of ID.

The Caucasian woman in front of me used her credit card and the clerk did not ask her for any form of ID.

MA Declaration #6
Blatantly avoiding my granddaughter and me in the grocery store.

MA Declaration #7
I have experienced microaggression when shopping with the clerk saying, "You do know the price, right?"

MA Declaration #8

I decided to visit a major department store in the San Diego area (Robinson Mays) dressed in jeans and a brown hoodie, just browsing the store. I noticed one of the sales associates (a White woman) following and watching me in the store. As I moved, so did she. She wasn't very good at hiding her intent. After several minutes of watching her watch me, I politely walked over and asked a question about an item. I thanked her for her assistance. Then I asked if she would be working the following day because I wanted to return and purchase the item that I had asked her about and make sure she got the sale. She said that she would be there on the following day.

So, I returned the next day dressed in business attire and noticed the different treatment I received from the same woman. She acknowledged my presence in the store and kept doing her work without following me around the store. When I approached her with that same item, I got a different response. I then identified myself as being the same Black woman she talked with the day before and how I had observed her watching me and the difference in her attitude towards me from one day to the other because of how I looked. I was bold enough to share with her that she needed to be cautious about how she stereotyped Black people because of the way that they are dressed.

MA Declaration #9

I stand around waiting while the employees help the White customers first.

MA Declaration #10

The clerk is checking out three White people in front of me and never once did she ask them for ID. When I get to the front, she asked me for my ID.

The "N" Word

MA Declaration #1

My high school in Mississippi had everything separated between Black and White. We had separate buses, separate class officers (i.e., a Black class president and a White class president), separate proms, etc. The only

34

thing not segregated was the classrooms. I was raised in California and wasn't used to this. When a White girl and I tried to hang together outside of class, the Whites started teasing her and calling her a "nigger lover." We had to stop hanging out so she wouldn't get bullied.

MA Declaration #2
I've been called a nigger, monkey, and a coon.

MA Declaration #3
Once, after investigating a complaint involving the accusation of a teacher's use of the "N" word during class time, a union leader stated to my supervisor, "How do you think it made the accused feel with CJ questioning him about using the "N" word? She made him feel uncomfortable." It was proven by a preponderance of evidence that the complaint was sustained. Eventually, the teacher submitted a complaint against me regarding the interview process, even though I was nothing but professional and respectful.

MA Declaration #4
I once had a patient ask me, "Who did your nose?"

MA Declaration #5
I had a patient call me a nigger and refused to let me help her even though she was clearly in pain.

MA Declaration #6
Walking across the road to my cousin's house to play, I could encounter at any moment White kids yelling "nigger" at me. I hated it.

MA Declaration #7
Since being a police officer, there have been plenty of times that I've been called a "nigger" by some civilian I'm dealing with. I deal with it by smiling and laughing because I'm usually arresting the person and their words don't affect me at all.

MA Declaration #8
"I don't understand why I can't use the "N" word when I hear Black people saying it all the time!"

MA Declaration #9
"Calling a Black person [nigger] isn't a bad thing is it?"

MA Declaration #10
"I was raised around Black people and it's a "term of endearment" even from a White person. I mean, as long as we're amongst our friends."

MA Declaration #11
"My parents used the "N" word on a daily basis to describe Black people. I didn't like it, but they're my parents."

Who's in Charge?

MA Declaration #1
I was the first Black assigned to be principal at Santiago High School in the Corona Norco Unified School District. This was a predominantly White high school in a middle- to high-income community in Riverside County. My assistant principal team included four White males. During many nights of sports supervision, we'd all carpool to the away games to assist with oversight of our students. On more than a few occasions, the opposing school's admin would walk over to greet us and more often than not mistake one of my White admin team members as the principal and completely bypass me, assuming I was a subordinate.

At first, our team would quickly correct them, but after it continued to occur at other away activities, I asked them not to correct the opposing admin and just go with it. It was fun for me and the team and later when I'd see that admin team at a regional event the embarrassment on their faces was priceless when they realized that I was actually the principal of that high performing, majority White high school. I was angry when it first began to occur, but decided to have some fun with others' assumptions and blatant disregard, which I interpreted as "there's no way this Black man could be the principal of that school!"

MA Declaration #2
As the Dean, I often meet with students for a variety of meetings. I was the first to arrive for the meeting then the students started coming in together. After the last student stepped in, I started the meeting. One student spoke up and said, "Shouldn't we wait for the Dean to arrive?"

MA Declaration #3
I introduced myself as the manager after a disgruntled customer asked for a manager. When she saw me, she said, I asked for a manager! I respectfully said, "I am the manager." She said, "That's okay, what's the number to your corporate office so I can speak to someone in charge!"

Workplace

MA Declaration #1
Early in my professional career, I experienced a situation that can be labeled as a microaggression. I prepared myself academically and gained significant workplace experience. I shared my career goals with my then supervisor who expressed support. I continued to apply for one job after another, frequently gaining interviews. However, I was not hired. I would follow up with the normal "how can I improve, what can I do in order to become much more competitive?" Frequently, I heard, "You did an excellent job." Finally, after two years of trying, I was hired as a mid-level supervisor. I continued to grow and flourish, and was promoted and hired into higher-level positions. Ten years ago, I ran into that supervisor in a big box store. She stopped me and proceeded to express how proud she was to read about my accomplishments and how successful I had become. What came next was not a surprise. She said, "I am so happy that my actions did not keep you from succeeding. I did not want to lose you in the department; therefore, I did not give you a good reference." What she did not know and I did not share with her, the person that finally offered me a position, shared that information with me. That person recognized the quality of my work and hired me anyway. That is one of the reasons I really recommend that young professionals check their references and do follow up.

MA Declaration #2

I am the first person of any color to supervise my division consisting primarily of old White men, one White woman, and one Latino woman. The men repeatedly go out of their way to tell me I'm doing a good job while simultaneously thwarting my authority.

MA Declaration #3

Negative comments downgrading my success on a weekly basis.

MA Declaration #4

A supervisor purchased a new car. The car happened to be black and she asked me if she should get personalized plates. She proceeded to ask me, the only person of color in the communication center, whether I thought "Tar Baby" would be cute. I asked her if she thought that was okay. Her response was, "Because my car is black." I guess that was her story and she was sticking to it.

MA Declaration #5

When I was sixteen, in Riverside, I saw a job announcement for a salesperson at a dress shop I frequented often. It was my 'go to' dress store. I called and made an appointment for an interview. The woman on the phone told me to come right down and they would interview me. I was getting dressed and my mother said, "Irene, don't get your hopes up." I said, "Why, they told me to come right down?" She again said, "Don't count on it." I was not to be discouraged and went for the interview. When I walked into the store, a lady said, "May I help you?" I stated that I had come for the interview for the salesperson job. She looked at me and said, "Oh, wait a minute." It took her awhile to come back, but when she did, she stated, "I'm sorry but the job has been filled." I looked at her stunned! I said, "I just called no more than an hour ago!" She stated there must have been some kind of mix up because the job was filled. That was my first disappointment in humanity and fairness.

MA Declaration #6

While working my first job as a new college graduate, as a recruiter for a placement firm, I encountered a young White woman co-worker with a stuck up attitude to everyone in the office. She once said that while one of her girlfriends was Black, she wasn't really Black because her skin was fairer and her eyes were lighter. I pondered her comment and reduced it to what stuck out as someone who was very limited in their cultural experience. She often exuded levels of diva-ism that struck me as odd as well since she accepted being in an abusive relationship, which degraded her being. She soon quit the job to aspire in another field. No one in our office missed her poor attitude and self-serving commentary. Note: the rest of the office staff was also White.

MA Declaration #7
Many times, during hiring interviews for teachers and other school staff, preference was given to Whites, without valid justification based on qualifications and/or experience. I had to remain firm in making sure this did not occur and that all candidates were fairly evaluated.

MA Declaration #8
My experience with microaggression racism happened while working in radio. There was a Hispanic manager who worked for the owner of the station who literally thought and acted as if Black people were contaminated, to the degree that he would actually walk down the hall spraying Lysol when we were present. One day, I decided to touch his arm and he freaked out. On another thought, I think that his behavior could have been attributed to a mental disorder regarding his perception of African Americans.

MA Declaration #9
Hiring managers assuming that I would look different from the name on my resume.

MA Declaration #10
I was told that Black engineers get paid less than White engineers. I didn't believe it. I worked with salaries, and never thought to look at Black vs. White salaries. I was so upset, I couldn't believe what I was looking at... it was true. Black employees with a Master's Degree were paid 10 to 15% less than their White counterparts with a Bachelor's Degree. I was so upset and hurt because I am Black and the best at what I do at the company

where I work. I was selected to manage troubled subcontracts for the other White females while they pretended to manage my subcontracts and take credit for my efforts.

MA Declaration #11

I'm responsible for Commissioning and Qualification (C&Q) of a new cell therapy manufacturing facility for my employer. C&Q is a specific phase of the project where we execute documented testing to ensure our systems are ready to start manufacturing medicine for our patients. As you can imagine, this requires a lot of attention to detail. The FDA reviews our work prior to approving drugs for sale. In my role, I interface with a User Team (I'm on the Project Team). The User Team is made up of employees who will work at the site once the building, equipment installation, and testing are complete. As a Principal Engineer, I have significant experience in this area and was excited for this project. At the beginning of this year, I walked into a standing meeting with the User Team and a colleague said that he'd feel more comfortable if my contractors represented the Project Team rather than me. I took two days off before the holidays and two days after, during which time I had my contractors cover a few meetings in my absence. Apparently, this was enough to prove my White and Latino male contractors, who work for me and for whom I direct their daily tasks, were more qualified to participate in the discussion than I was.

MA Declaration #12

Reporting to Human Resources, incidents that I felt were racially motivated by my boss at my second job in IT after graduating college. Many times, my complaints went unnoticed.

MA Declaration #13

Finding out that my co-workers referred to me as "the one who looks like a monkey" while describing who I was.

MA Declaration #14

When I started in my new position in my current district, the White person in the room, who was supposed to be the person "showing me the ropes" on the job, was very interested in where I lived in San Jose. I thought that was an extremely odd question to ask me on the day in which I was asked to get my materials. In hindsight, I realized the White person was trying to 'size me up' and determine the worth she was going to place on me based on my living location.

MA Declaration #15

I forgot that I was to attend a meeting. I "dressed down" on Friday, like many educators in our school building do. A White female advocate happened to be attending that meeting and when I introduced myself as the school psychologist, she looked me up and down in utter disgust. Of course, I knew I was not dressed to 'meeting' standards; however, I was not going to let that impact my meeting attendance. During the meeting, another psychologist that sounded like a White male was on the phone and team members discussed ways in which we could assist the student being discussed. I gave my input, and the White male echoed my sentiments stating, "I don't know who that was, but that was really good and I agree with her." Thereafter, the White woman's demeanor towards me COMPLETELY AND INSTANTLY SHIFTED.

MA Declaration #16

As Senior Counsel managing litigation for my company, I had to review and sometimes correct memoranda and briefs written by outside attorneys for my company. Generally, since I was the client and knew the company better than the outside attorneys, my input was valued. However, one White male junior associate (with far less experience than I had), did not appreciate my changes to the memo he wrote and argued that his version should prevail "as he graduated from Stanford Law School." I told him that I too graduated from Stanford Law School and that regardless, I was paying the bill and he would make the changes I recommended. I also spoke to the firm partner about him and had him removed from all my company cases. He left (or was asked to leave) the firm soon after.

MA Declaration #17

Often, when going to court for a hearing, when I tried to walk up beyond the bar to the counsel tables, I would be stopped by the bailiff or the court clerk and told "Attorneys only up here." I would wearily say, "I am an attorney" as I hefted my large litigation bag onto the table.

MA Declaration #18

When attending regional office meetings for my company as the legal representative, I frequently was asked to go get coffee or make copies. I usually informed the requestor that [name of Company] doesn't pay its attorneys to make coffee and that ended the discussion.

MA Declaration #19

Asked upon to respond or speak on behalf of African American issues when everyone should be champions of equity.

MA Declaration #20

Regularly, in meetings with administrative leadership, my comments are ignored or brushed aside. However, a White woman or model minority Asian will say the same thing and it suddenly is a "really good idea."

MA Declaration #21

I was raised in St. Louis, MO, where racism was 'on the table.' Blacks didn't like Whites and vice versa. We both knew it; however, we still worked together and went to school together but didn't acknowledge our individual prejudices verbally. When I was in middle school, my family moved to San Diego. Racism was totally different. It was 'undercover.' As a light-skinned Black girl, I was technically not a threat. I was raised to not let my first thought (if I was being mistreated) be, "All White people are not me, look at yourself, first." So, I overlooked a lot of things growing up thinking possibly, maybe, there was something I was doing wrong. I transferred to a department at my current job/company where after transferring for more opportunity, the White man that hired me was the number one racist in the company.

A White young lady was hired at the exact same time I was hired (same start date, same position). I began to see that she was awarded a lot of extra training and opportunities that I was also requesting. I was always told, "Not yet, we need you where you are, maybe later." That happened for three years. I was getting more and more frustrated every time I saw them giving her opportunities that I was not given. During a particular event, I walked into the break room full of White men, and there were several pictures of nooses on the table. The room was quiet as I walked in. I felt very uncomfortable and exited the room. I never mentioned it to anyone because I assumed that's what they do. I'm learning now that someone did complain to upper management, but nothing was done. I was never involved in a fact-finding meeting. After being there for three years, I interviewed and was offered a promotion to another department. (I still believe to this day that if I would have said something, there would have been retaliation, and I wouldn't have received a promotion). After I left the department, I looked back in retrospect, and realized all of the "NO's" and "Wait's" and "Be Patient's" were actually racism that I allowed them to get away with. Mainly, because I didn't recognize it was racism and I was afraid to say something about the nooses.

You Are Different

MA Declaration #1
A co-worker described a Black colleague as being too dark and then apologized to me by saying I was different. Subsequently, the same person also said (after I'd applied for a promotional opportunity) that they hoped the person promoted would not be a Black person. When I replied that I applied for the position, they stated, "Well, I didn't mean you."

MA Declaration #2
When I first moved from Oakland to Manteca, I was asked on a consistent basis, "How do you wash your hair?"

MA Declaration #3
"Why do you speak that way?"

MA Declaration #4
"You're pretty for a black girl!"

MA Declaration #5
A co-worker told me, "Sometimes I forget that you are Black. You are just like one of us." She is Hispanic, 90% of my co-workers are.

MA Declaration #6
I've been called, "A credit to my race."

You Don't Belong Here

MA Declaration #1
I was selected to be superintendent in an isolated mountain community in CA. The board reported that my skills matched their needs and that I was hands down the most qualified candidate in the pool of applicants. I moved to the community and met every item on the board and community member's wishlist within a few months. I submitted all district required reports, trained the board, and used data to inform everyone. Entitled staff members that informally ran the district prior to my hiring didn't want me there. This person convened a team to take me down. They met off the record behind the scenes to cultivate a following in favor of removing me. Someone made a CPS report based on a student stating that I said something inappropriate to a SPED student. This was unfounded and easily shown to be untrue by the cameras in the setting where this matter was alleged to have happened.

My parking space was blocked every morning by parents to upset me. I had the space labeled and then people put it out that I thought I was better than everyone. Random community members came onto the campus without signing in to observe, report, and so call to spend quality time with a relative. When this practice was rerouted to follow safety procedures with a visitor procedure the next few board meetings were packed with random people angrily sharing how they were made to feel unwanted and that I was militant.

All while these acquisitions and harassment was happening I was bringing in professional development to teachers, growing parent engagement, providing student events that were on a wishlist, and making connections with students from grades K-8. Students would hug me and leave their parents at school events to hang out with me. The community didn't have many African Americans and they clearly were uncomfortable with me amongst them. I quit and left because I felt unsafe.

MA Declaration #2
I've lived in the same predominantly White neighborhood for seventeen years and still get long obvious stares when I'm walking around the

neighborhood (even from people in their cars) as if I am out of place and don't belong in the neighborhood.

MA Declaration #3

At my first law firm job, during one of our first firm attorney lunches, they went around the table asking all the new attorneys "what their fathers did for a living." I was the only Black attorney working in that office and one of a handful of female attorneys. It immediately struck me that they only asked about the fathers (as if the mothers didn't work). They went around the table and the replies prior to mine were, "My father is a Senior VP at [one of the firm's largest clients]," "My father owns a jewelry store," "My father is an attorney." When I said that my father was an LA City garbage collector, the room erupted into laughter and someone said, "No, what does he really do?" I repeated my answer. There was an embarrassing silence and even worse, all afternoon, firm partners kept coming to my office asking me to relive what happened and make a "list" of everyone who laughed.

MA Declaration #4

Attending UCI and living in Orange County, I am very familiar with South Coast Plaza and Fashion Island, but no matter how nicely I am dressed, whether in St. John or jeans, I am followed around in almost every store I shop in. I usually just turn around and ask the salesperson to find the item in my size or just say "Can I help you?"

Sometimes I get disgusted and just leave, deciding not to spend my money in the store. Also, I have often been asked by store employees, when paying by credit card, "How/where did you get this card?" Depending on my mood, sometimes I will say "Because I don't work at _____" (fill in the name of the store).

"You People"

MA Declaration #1

I had a boss (Cambodian woman) raised in Oakland tell me we needed to hire more people like us from the hood to work in our clinic. Because of race and my demographic of growing up in a poorer area, she assumed that I was aggressive and would fight if needed.

MA Declaration #2
White people trying to show me how cool they were because they could "talk Black."

MA Declaration #3
I've been told I sounded/acted White (by both Black and White people).

MA Declaration #4
As an African American professional in the educational field, I have often had to deal with people's subtle racism (i.e., you are so articulate, and you are well spoken).

MA Declaration #5
"But if your people would not be so loud, aggressive, angry, defensive…"

MA Declaration #6
"Get over it. Forget about slavery; that was in the past!"

MA Declaration #7
Told stories of my friend's parents who don't like Black people because they had a "bad experience" once.

A MOMENT TO REFLECT

Stop, relax, close your eyes, take a deep breath, reflect, and ask yourself the following questions…

1. Which microaggression declarations stood out the most for you and why?

2. What was the lesson(s) learned, if any?

3. If you identified a microaggression declaration that you related to, what could you have done differently?

4. Which person comes to mind when you identified with the declaration?

5. What is your plan of action to rectify this situation?

6. Do you believe it can be resolved?

7. Are you willing to pick up the phone, send an email or text message, or use a virtual platform to have an exchange of dialogue with the person?

8. Consider using the Shawn E. Model: "Close our eyes, take a deep breath, reflect, and recognize that everything will be alright!"

9. Consider relying on the model that Dr. Darlene V. Griffin Willis uses, which is God's scripture, "…quick to listen, slow to speak, and slow to anger" (See James 1:19).

10. Are you willing to try applying the Willis A^3 Model (acknowledge, accept, and apologize)? If the answer is yes…go for it! If the answer is that you are not ready…keep reflecting, re-reading, praying, meditating and searching to find the best resolution for you!

BLATANT RACISM

BLATANT RACISM TESTIMONIES

"Overt, obvious, and almost always meant to harm.
Can lead to mental and physical injury, violent destruction, or
even death."

Airlines

Testimony #1
Title/Area of Expertise: Career/Personal Coaching and Development
Recently while boarding a Southwest flight, my daughter asked a question. I had her ask the attendant who responded with, "Now don't get in trouble." I politely educated her on using appropriate language when talking to little Black children given the political climate. She proceeded to tell me that she would've said the same thing to "a purple, green, or blue child." I then explained that there are no purple, green, or blue children present, but there was a little Black child that could then internalize being accused of potentially getting in trouble.

Recommendations/Resolutions/Lessons Learned
I would recommend that they befriend Black and/or Brown friends. Become invested in the betterment of ALL mankind and become aware of internal/implicit biases. Do not internalize the actions of ignorant people. Learn and recognize your worth. Find pride in who you are.

Testimony #2
Title/Area of Expertise: Retired Veteran
While employed at World Airways Inc., in the 1970s, out of Oakland, CA, I was hired as an aircraft mechanic and worked there for eighteen years. I was promoted to lead mechanic, became a union shop steward, then chief steward, and then became a foreman, and eventually the president of the federal credit union. Early on, as a mechanic, I witnessed overt discrimination throughout the company. They included lack of hiring and underpayment to Black employees who were disrespected and treated unfairly due to our color.

Recommendations/Resolutions/Lessons Learned
I organized the minority workers forming a group called "MEWARE" (Minority Employees Working and Resisting Exploitation) and had several members sign the letter to prevent myself from being fired. I then filed charges with the EEOC (Equal Employment Opportunity Commission) citing discrimination and violations of title V11. of the Civil Rights Act of 1964, as well as order four of the affirmative action plan. An investigating commission was assigned to our case and for six months,

they completed facts and statistics that supported our claim. We won! A conciliation commission was established to bring all parties together for the purpose of negotiating a settlement. That is why I was elected president of the World Airways Federal Credit Union and was the only minority of the twelve-member board that consisted of vice presidents and department heads, all White. In my new role, I continued to fight workplace discrimination because I was exposed to redlining and other forms of biases such as the Credit Committee not approving loans for buying property but would approve car loans because they knew if there was a missed payment they would repossess and resell.

Testimony #3
Title/Area of Expertise: Reverend/Leadership
Three years ago, I was flying and all the Brown and Black people were literally pulled out of the line to get onto the airplane for "random screening." Our names were read out over the loudspeaker to confirm our presence in the "random" group. We were held until the lobby was empty and then released onto the plane without any further questioning.

Recommendations/Resolutions/Lessons Learned
There were no recommendations, resolutions, or lessons learned.

Arts

Testimony #1
Title/Area of Expertise: Artist
In 2004, the breast cancer awareness sculpture that I created for my mother's struggle with the disease, won the "Judge's Choice" award at the Valley Sculpture Artists Competition. Normally, the Best of Show art piece is displayed in the First Gallery of the Sacramento Fine Arts Center, in a place of honor, but mine was in the Second Gallery, positioned so low that people couldn't see it.

I found this out on the night of the awards ceremony. I was furious and embarrassed that my friends and family had to witness my disgrace, but I was too flummoxed to stand up for myself and my art to make a ruckus that night.

Recommendations/Resolutions/Lessons Learned
I should have let my Black Woman voice come out, but I didn't. I left the event as soon as the awards were issued. Every time I saw the head of that event, I would glare at her, my blood pressure soaring. It ate at me for fifteen years.

This year I wrote an email to the perpetrator about how demeaned I felt from her treatment of me, especially since I had taken the day off work to help her manage the judging process. I burned a printed copy of the email, hoping to expunge it from my memory. She has not responded. I should have addressed the slight immediately on the night of the awards ceremony.

Testimony #2
Title/Area of Expertise: Education
A memory surfaced recently of me and my sister being the only Black girls in an advanced ballet class for several years, in which all the White girls in the class were promoted to pointe, while we were not. When we asked why, we were told that Black people's bodies were not suitable for classical ballet. She went on to state that Black people had flat feet and that their body type was not that of a ballerina.

Recommendations/Resolutions/Lessons Learned
The learning moment for me was the different way my sister and I handled the teacher's racist words and actions. After a few more attempts of being promoted to pointe and not being awarded that which I deserved, I quit ballet. My sister, however, stayed in the class.

Two months later, our ballet teacher took a month-long leave. During that month, a new ballet teacher was assigned to the class. The new teacher complimented my sister on her technique and how she was a top ballerina. My sister shared that she was not on pointe. The teacher put her through the assessment process to be awarded to the status of a pointe ballerina.

When the original ballet teacher returned she treated my sister poorly, but she stayed with it. I learned that in the same situation people make different decisions in how to handle racist situations.

Banking/Financial

Testimony #1
Title/Area of Expertise: Underwriter/Mortgage Banking
I was a young bank teller and I was the only teller that was not White and a White man refused to come to my teller window. When I said I was available to help him with his bank transaction, he stated, "I don't want a nigger helping me" and he proceeded to wait until a White teller was available. I was young and thought I would ignore him. It was ultimately his loss as he waited a very long time before someone would help him, because everyone in the bank heard his comment.

Recommendations/Resolutions/Lessons Learned
There was no resolution, but definitely a learning moment. I was satisfied with the outcome as I didn't want to help someone with that type of hate that had no basis. He didn't know me; he made a judgment based on the color of my skin. His loss.

Bi-Racial

Testimony # 1
Title/Area of Expertise: Teacher
My earliest memories of starting to really notice or even understand racism started when I was in the first grade. Teachers and peers would ask me if my mom was really my mom because she was not the same complexion as me. My mom is Mexican and has lighter skin than me and that would always make people question if she was my real mom. The same reaction occurred when people found out how my sister looked. She also has light skin and people would ask, "Do you have the same parents?" To this day, I get asked the same question. It's crazy to think that people have a hard time understanding that we have the same parents, but different skin tones. Peers in elementary school up until high school would say, "You're not really Mexican because you don't speak Spanish" or "you're not really Black because you don't have nappy hair." Growing up, my peers and community consisted of mostly Mexicans and there were times when I felt like I didn't fit in because I didn't speak the language or because, according to society, my hair didn't look "Black."

When people found out that I was [multi-racial] I would always get asked, "Well, which one do you consider yourself more of?" or "If you had to choose a side, which one would you pick?" I never knew how to answer those questions and now, being older, I realize how insane those questions were. But what really helped me deal with these experiences as a child was being connected to both sides. I spent most of my time with my mom's side of the family because they all lived in the same city. So, I grew up being really close to them. My father's side I didn't see as much, but I knew who they were. My dad always told stories about his childhood and family. I would spend holidays like Thanksgiving with his side of the family, which allowed me to learn more about my Blackness. I believed that really helped me deal with the questions and statements I would get from my peers because I had a relationship with both sides. It was probably not until college when I took an African Studies class and was surrounded with Black people, when I really started feeling confident and comfortable with who I am. Most recently as an adult, I experienced a White man telling me, "You're hot for a Black girl."

Recommendations/Resolutions/Lessons Learned
Growing up in a community where I was one of the only Black girls, I guess I can't really blame my peers for questioning me about my race because I was the only [multi-racial] girl they knew. As crazy as their questions were, I'm also glad they asked because it opened up conversation. Although I didn't know exactly what to say, it prepared me to get to know myself better and learn more, so next time someone asks me, I know what to say. Thankfully, as we grew up, many of my peers didn't see me as the Black girl at school anymore. For the White man who made the comment about me being cute for a Black girl, I responded to him and said, "Is that supposed to be a compliment? Because it's not." He was surprised with my response and didn't know what to say after. It wasn't a place that would allow me to further explain how that comment was offensive, so I walked away.

Testimony # 2
Title/Area of Expertise: Studying to be an Actuary
I was about 26 or 27, and I was dating a 21/22 year old White woman (Puerto Rican/Italian mix, but she passed for White and claimed it). She kept in contact with boyfriends from her past as friends, just as I had done with many girlfriends from mine. One particular ex-boyfriend caught wind of

who I was, and he said to her, "You're dating a nigger? Gross!" I understand people say whatever they want when they are disappointed, but it has to stem from a real place of disrespect. How I handled it: I went on Facebook and found him. I then went to his friend's house and found all the Black people I could find. I told each one I saw what he'd said. All but one appreciated my honesty. The one in particular that stood out said, in so many words, that he said it to me and did not say it to him and that I shouldn't be "trying to break up family." So that Black man was the only one to stand up for him, but they live in a small town in the sticks, and I understand his type of mentality.

Recommendations/Resolutions/Lessons Learned
There was no grand resolution. There were several learning moments, however. I learned that some Black people will defend a racist White person despite claims of overt racism. I also learned that, coming from a privileged background, I was more enraged/affected by hearing the word directed at me than I should have allowed. I learned that I did not truly see the world for what it is–imperfect. I don't think there was anything more that could have been done. It would have been my word against his. I had been in and out of the hospital during this time due to drug use, so my credibility had taken a hit. I'm not sure what type of therapy one needs to not be racist. I've grown up with many diverse influences around a diverse group of people. I've put in thousands of hours of volunteer work. In my teen years, I worked in the service industry waiting tables. I've also had the privilege of many different opportunities that many around me didn't have. For me, being nonracist comes from my upbringing and wanting good for those around me.

Churches/Spirituality

Testimony #1
Title/Area of Expertise: Retired
In California, at church when another friend invited me to hear a speaker. I knew they were going to have a potluck and my friends invited me to go and get some food. The current president, a young White woman, told me, "You don't belong here." I just went back to the table and they asked me what happened. A past president went back and asked, "Why wasn't she served?" He informed her that I had been a member for over 50 years. The current president said that while they were setting up, a homeless person came by and being the only Black person there, she assumed I was homeless.

Recommendations/Resolutions/Lessons Learned
I still go back and visit every now and then but I will remember that incident that just happened a couple of years ago. She'll always remember it as well because every time she sees me, she goes out of her way to speak and be pleasant.

Testimony #2
Title/Area of Expertise: Educator
Worshipping in a White congregation with few Blacks as members has been an experience. Most are loving, but many look at me as if I don't belong there. If I say "amen" out loud or do a "call and response," I feel stares from others.

Recommendations/Resolutions/Lessons Learned
I've accepted that I have to be who God wants me to be and continue to give God all the glory, despite how others may feel. I've learned to tune out the noise and just focus on what I came to do and that's to praise God!

Civic Organizations

Testimony # 1
Title/Area of Expertise: Education/Legal Administration
When my family and I first moved to Diamond Bar and I signed my daughters up for Girl Scouts, I was told the troop was closed. A neighbor who moved in a week before school started signed her daughter up in the troop where I was told it was closed. I later found out it was closed to Blacks.

Recommendations/Resolutions/Lessons Learned
I started my own Girl Scout troop. It should never have happened. The adult involved should have been suspended from being a troop leader. The troop should have been disbanded. It is important to get all the facts and due diligence before generalizing about someone based on one's race or ethnicity.

Dining/Restaurants

Testimony # 1
Title/Area of Expertise: Artist
My family and I often felt we were being targeted when we would go out to eat, whether breakfast, lunch, or dinner, simple or fancy, it was always the same welcome scene. We'd stroll into a restaurant, café, or eatery and the hostess would direct us to a table or hand us off to a server to seat us.

Either way, they would pass empty table sections to escort us to the very back, near the bathroom, the drink station, or the noisy kitchen area. Of course, we'd nicely request to sit in a front area we'd observed enroute to the back, and they would oblige. Most times my husband remarked, "It's like y'all are trained to seat Blacks in the back." They would reply, "No Sir," looking like they just swallowed something uncomfortable.

I remember several times we stood midway in the restaurant and watched the hostess or server walk to the back without us! When they turned around, we'd show them where we wanted to sit. Again, they said ok. So why weren't we given that seating choice in the beginning?

Recommendations/Resolutions/Lessons Learned
We realized this would happen no matter where we went or how we were dressed, whether with our kids or out as a couple. We decided to select our table in the beginning, asking for a booth or a window seat near the front, and they obliged. I'd express to them what I felt about their comments or actions being perceived as racist. And, give them an example of how to avoid their actions of appearing as racist.

Testimony # 2
Title/Area of Expertise: Educator
In 1972 at a Miss North Carolina Pageant Workshop, in Asheboro, N.C., I went into a restaurant with a group of other contestants and their chaperones during our lunch break. The other chaperones and their contestants went inside, and were seated. My Caucasian female chaperone was told that she could be seated, but I could not, as they did not "serve Blacks inside the restaurant."

Recommendations/Resolutions/Lessons Learned
My female Caucasian chaperone said, "That is okay! We do not eat Black people." She took my hand and we left. She was very embarrassed and I was very angry. We ate crackers and a soda at a nearby gas station sitting in the car. We went back to the afternoon session, my chaperone reported what had happened, and the workshop organizers were apologetic to us and asked if they could get us lunch. I was never made aware of anything that was done to change that situation. I believe that workshop organizers should have provided us with lunch or they should have cleared the way for all of us with the restaurant. I was the only Black contestant. That incident taught me to always push the envelope, and ask "Why?" when I encounter a situation that I feel is unfair or degrading.

Testimony #3
Title/Area of Expertise: Executive Leadership/Education
A recent blatant experience was at a nice restaurant. A waiter refused to serve my family because we were Black. I didn't know this was the reason at first, but after not being served, not even water, for a half hour, I went to ask questions. I overheard the server explaining to the manager that she didn't want to serve a table of "broke-ass Black people... why are they even here." I heard the manager tell her to serve us for 15 minutes until someone else came back and he'd switch them. When the manager walked out and saw me, he was stunned and immediately apologized. I told him that we would not be spending our money at an establishment that tolerated such racism. I handled the situation by 1) leaving, 2) contacting LegalShield and allowing an attorney to handle the rest, and 3) spending our money at a restaurant that welcomed us.

Recommendations/Resolutions/Lessons Learned
I try to make room for learning moments. It's a part of my nature. But sometimes it's exhausting, as it puts the onus of change on the victim and that's weighty. I'm at a stage now where most things I forward to an attorney to handle for resolution, which is one reason why I believe every person of color should have LegalShield coverage. It has helped me so much. And sometimes, I have been able to engage in restorative conversations. My advice would be to know and be confident in who you are. Consider and use your resources. Never silence or shield your voice. Activate your faith. And, be an agent of change. I would advise a racist to do the self-work of exploring their lenses, implicit biases, and assumptions, and commit to practicing the antithesis.

Driving While Black

Testimony # 1
Title/Area of Expertise: Educator
A White driver being in a hurry behind me at the stop sign once yelled out to me, "Damn nigger you're fucking slow and dumb!" I got out of my car and yelled back, "I'm also 6'8" with a bad crack ass cracker problem!" He quickly changed his tone and apologized.

Recommendations/Resolutions/Lessons Learned
Depending on how much energy I have, I always try to turn racial opportunities to teachable moments at work. It's a moment of clarity for my White co-workers. I try to teach them why it is important to see color in society. They have to be willing to unlearn and then relearn the truth about ethnicities. #BlackLivesMatter

Testimony # 2
Title/Area of Expertise: PhD Candidate
I have been routinely pulled over and detained by the Orange County Sheriff's Department while walking home. I have been racially profiled and followed by police more times than I can count both on and off of UCI's campus. Below is a summary of just a few of the times I have been unlawfully profiled by law enforcement:

Before college:
1. (San Rafael) Pulled over driving out of the back gate of the prison with dad, by Twin City PD headed for Sacramento. After verifying I was not on parole, probation, or had any outstanding warrants, they let us off with a warning because pops did not have a seatbelt on.
2. (Oakland) Pulled from the back seat while riding with HS classmates (White and Asian dudes) in Oakland to shoot a video on police corruption in America (the irony). After verifying I was not on parole, probation, or had any outstanding warrants (me, the passenger in the back seat), they let us off with a warning for not having a front license plate.
3. (Marin) Stopped by CHP, and two Twin City police officers while changing a spare tire after the wheel fell off on the way home. After

verifying I was not on parole, probation, or had any outstanding warrants they then watched as I changed my tire (all 6 of them).

In College at UCI:

4. (Oakley) While driving home from Black Bear Diner in Oakley with pops, I was stopped by the Oakley Police gang task force unit for suspicion of DUI. A field sobriety test was performed. I passed, but I was detained until they proved my identity and that I was not on parole, probation, or had any outstanding warrants.

5. (On campus) While studying in MSTB with Vatche Donikian, we were detained then escorted out of the building by UCI police and the on-duty supervisor.

6. (On campus) Walking out of the Anteater parking structure with Lamar Washington and Vatche Donikian, we were detained by UCI PD until our identities were checked after someone called the police to report three suspicious individuals (textbooks and back packs in hand).

7. (On campus) While waiting outside of a professor's office in NFCRC for his office hours, which he was late to! UCI police attempted to detain me after someone called to say I matched the description of an individual they were looking for. Luckily, my professor intervened before officers could do anything.

8. (Berkley) While home on college break, after leaving San Pablo Park watching my cousins softball game, I was pulled over on Sacramento St. and Ashby. After verifying I was not on parole, probation, or had any outstanding warrants, I was let go with a warning for having tinted windows.

9. (Lake Forest) While walking home to my apartment, OC Sheriff Deputy, Pablo Alverez, pulled me over and detained me because in his words, "I looked like a good stop."

10. (Lake Forest) While walking home, OC Sheriff's Department deputy and on-call SGT followed me with an alley light trained on me as I walked home on the sidewalk before them detaining me to verify my identity.

11. (Lake Forest) While walking home on the sidewalk, a female OC deputy detained me until she could verify my identity. She threatened to take me in for fingerprinting because she did not believe my driver's license was a valid ID. She then let me off with a warning for jaywalking.

12. After scheduling a police ride-along with Lake Forest OC Sheriff's Department, in an attempt to force community policing by getting to know the individuals that routinely detain me, I was detained in the parking lot by the very officer I was supposed to be riding along with that night.
13. On 6/11/20, picking up Dr. Adams from John Wayne Airport, I was pulled over after parking. [The officer] told me my headlight was out, my windows were not legal, and I had a warrant under my name. After running ID, they let me off with a warning for the tints and it turns out none of my headlights were out, plus it was 6:45 p.m., broad daylight outside (Irvine PD stopped me). After this stop, I just quit counting…

Recommendations/Resolutions/Lessons Learned

I learned to not make any sudden movements and remain calm even if the officers are aggressive. I also find that showing my school ID helps deescalate the situation. I learned that, in general as a Black man, the assumption taken by the police is almost always that you are a threat and so the onus is going to be on you to prove you are a law-abiding citizen. In almost all of the incidents I have had with police, I had not broken a law; therefore, I feel like there should not have been an interaction to start with. After attempting to file a police harassment complaint at city hall and the OC Sheriff's Department, I was told that they did not make police complaint forms. I was told by an OC Sheriff's Department SGT while trying to file a complaint that it was not "racial profiling" I was experiencing, but rather "criminal profiling."

Testimony # 3

Title/Area of Expertise: Declined to State

I try to avoid escalation, because so many times people will unjustly react out of fear creating a possibility of negative interaction with either them or the police. So, I try to just keep my mouth closed, and choose my battles.

Recommendations/Resolutions/Lessons Learned

I think [blatant racism] happens often, so you have to always be prepared for such an interaction. Remaining calm, and not allowing provocation to prevail is the best way to beat these types of interactions. I think empathy is the key. If one has to second guess if their comment is appropriate or not, it's probably not. We are living in a different time, and racist comments and jokes can literally ruin your life. I think this societal shift is good and will force some people who have been recently emboldened to correct their behavior. Ice Cube once suggested to "Check yaself, before ya wreck yaself."

Testimony #4
Title/Area of Expertise: Reverend/Leadership
Last Monday, I was pulled over at gunpoint while driving our foster child around to put him to sleep. No reason was given; no registration or identification was asked for. Just a flashlight and gun pointed in my direction before a tap on the window and a wave to move along were given.

Recommendations/Resolutions/Lessons Learned
Sometimes, as in the instance with getting pulled over, there is nothing that can be done. The structural authority is imbalanced and unless I have the time to start a movement, I am left with voting and other personal practices.

Education

Testimony # 1
Title/Area of Expertise: Retired Government
The year was 1975. I was 12 years old, living in South Central Los Angeles and was going to be attending San Fernando Valley for junior high school. I had to be bused to school and the busing program was PWT (Permit With Transportation). My older brother had attended Mulholland Jr. High too, but had already graduated. He reassured me I was going to like my new school.

The first day of school there were only two buses from Los Angeles, with most of us coming from South Central. Our new school was at least 90% Caucasian, 7% other, and 3% Black. It was the second day of the new school year. As we circled the drop off point in front of the administration building, we were welcomed with graffiti on the building: "NIGGERS GO HOME."

The principal, Mr. Sherry, held an assembly in the multi-purpose room that morning and spoke to the whole school. The administration building was scrubbed clean by the time we came out of the assembly.

Testimony #2
Title/Area of Expertise: Manager
While working at UC Berkeley, I was approved for a promotion during the same time the department leadership was changing. The new leadership consisted of two White women, who continued to deny the implementation of my promotion because, as they stated to me, they did not agree with the previous administration's decision. They also told me that they felt my new role's responsibilities were more in line with a White male department manager. I was informed by my direct report director, who was also a White woman that she was waiting for an explanation from Human Resources on how they determined I was qualified to be promoted to this new position.

Recommendations/Resolutions/Lessons Learned
After several months of no movement, I filed a complaint with EEOC and the promotion was handled within 30 days, including back pay. At the managerial staff meeting, my promotion was announced along with the fact that the White male manager had also been reclassified to the same position level as me.

Educate themselves on American History and how the U.S. constitution came to be written. Additionally, read information related to the treatment of Native Americans and African Americans from the moment slavery was introduced. Call them out on their racist ways - silence gives power.

Testimony #3
Title/Area of Expertise: Equity, Diversity & Inclusion
During the school year 2004-2005, I was the Dean of a predominately White, high socioeconomic high school in Southern California. After suspending a White male student for the second time, his mother came to my office, began berating me, and yelling profanities. She flew into an abusive rage, while in the presence of my White secretary and two White male students. Ultimately, she called me a "Fuckin' nigger."

Recommendations/Resolutions/Lessons Learned
Following the incident, I asked the administration was there any action I could take against the parent, but no one seemed able or willing to help. A week later, the other assistant principal mentioned that I could possibly file a restraining order against the parent, and I did. I also made sure to document the incident in the computer system and sent an email to the Superintendent detailing the incident the same day it occurred. In essence, there was really no resolution. I suggest that they partake in some sort of implicit bias training. Talk and intermingle with others who do not look like them and/or are not a part of their culture. Be empathetic, open to change/growth, willing to listen, and do not be afraid to ask questions about whether a particular behavior is offensive or racist. Be cognizant of what they are saying and doing. Do not make excuses whether the hurtful action was intentional or not. Do not assume one person speaks for an entire race.

Testimony #4
Title/Area of Expertise: Education Specialist
As a child growing up in the 1970s and early 1980s, the first memory I have of a blatantly racist incident was when I was in elementary school, first or second grade. I remember sitting alone at a table in the library; there were older boys, maybe fourth or fifth graders, at a table nearby. I remember one of the boys pretending (or actually trying) to catch flies. Finally, he told his friends they should move closer to me so that they would catch more flies because I was the color of "shit."

Recommendations/Resolutions/Lessons Learned
In the case of the boys in the library, they got in trouble for the noise they were making but never for the behaviors and comments imposed on me.

Testimony #5
Title/Area of Expertise: Education Specialist
I have another memory of being on a playground with my sister. She and I were the only two Black girls in the whole school. I remember a small group of girls approaching and asking her friends if she thought it was true that I (possibly) had a tail.

Recommendations/Resolutions/Lessons Learned
I never reported the comments made by the girls on the playground.

Testimony #6
Title/Area of Expertise: Education Specialist
While at Tuskegee, there were various moments of racism that made me nauseous. The casual acknowledgment of my presence by White townspeople as a "gal" and the rejection of services in an Auburn, Alabama, business because they didn't serve "our kind."

Recommendations/Resolutions/Lessons Learned
The behaviors in Tuskegee were never acknowledged or dealt with.

Testimony #7
Title/Area of Expertise: Community Worker
In high school, my sophomore year (1986), we attempted to start a Black Student Union. We had no Black faculty. We asked faculty members to sponsor our group, and received quite a few No's, not available, busy, etc. We finally received a 'Yes' from the drama teacher who happened to be a White female lesbian. As we advertised inviting students to join, we witnessed students mocking and pulling our signs down.

Recommendations/Resolutions/Lessons Learned
With my experience of church programs, I was able to produce the first Black History Program. All history teachers brought their students, we collaborated with the music teacher to have a choir singing the Black national anthem. We had everyone stand in acknowledgement. We played *The Eyes on the Prize*, which showed the civil rights movement, the atrocities of Emmett Till, etc.

Testimony #8
Title/Area of Expertise: Professor
I was being interviewed in a room with thirty department colleagues for a department chair position. The majority of my colleagues were White males along with a few White females. At the time, we had two Hispanic males, one Hispanic female, one Black male and two Black females. I was the third Black female. I was asked this ridiculous scenario and I told the group it was not a realistic question. After several minutes of back and forth, one older White guy screamed from the back of the room, ANSWER THE QUESTION!!! I locked eyes with my senior Black colleagues and took ten deep breaths and softly replied, "Well, if you are going to respond

like that, the answer is no." I did not receive enough votes for the department chair, but I am the associate department chair.

Recommendations/Resolutions/Lessons Learned
There was no resolution and when I discussed it with others in the department, I was told, "He does that to others, that's just his way!" My response was, "Let him know, the next time he raises his voice, I'm filing a grievance with the institution and the office of institutional equity."

Testimony #9
Title/Area of Expertise: Artist
I remember clearly being called "nigger" from the sidelines at a high school soccer game and seeing no consequences for it. (This incident took place at a high school but not in a learning capacity.)

Recommendations/Resolutions/Lessons Learned
Much of the bullying I experienced young, was never corrected. In fact, a lot of times I would be the one to get in trouble once I decided to stand up for myself. I believe teachers, role models, and authority figures should not just call out blatant forms of racism but also become more privy to the smaller forms that give way for serious injustices and encourage justification of inhumanity when it does occur.

Testimony #10
Title/Area of Expertise: Transportation Operations Manager
In the 1980s, while at the University of California Irvine, the Black Greek-lettered organizations planned a commemorative march from MASON Park back to the campus to commemorate the Martin Luther King, Jr. holiday. As the groups of us assembled with our signs and were headed back to UCI, a car of White males drove by us and yelled out of the window "NIGGERS!"

Recommendations/Resolutions/Lessons Learned
There were no resolutions or recommendations provided.

Testimony #11
Title/Area of Expertise: Retired School Administrator
I was one of the first African Americans to attend the University of North Texas.

Recommendations/Resolutions/Lessons Learned
We returned to the University many years later and the then president apologized to us for the way we were treated.

Testimony #12
Title/Area of Expertise: Educator
I can recall the first time I was called the N-word. I was in elementary school. We were at play practice and a person who I thought was a friend, called me the N-word. I took piano lessons from her. I was extra nice to her because she had leukemia. So many things ran through my head. I was shocked, angry, and my immediate response was to call the person a name and say something that would hurt her.

After having a conversation with my mom, she told me the proper way to handle the situation. She taught me how to not give that word power and told me that word meant an ignorant person. It didn't apply to me. She said that the word could apply to people of all races. It was just a word that was used to demoralize Black people. She told me to pray for her. This was one of my experiences where I began to realize I was not looked at the same as other people because of the color of my skin.

Recommendations/Resolutions/Lessons Learned
The very same person who called me the N-word changed her way of thinking. The last time I saw her, I was home one summer on break from college. She was actually happy to see me. We had a long conversation about how life was treating us.

Testimony #13
Title/Area of Expertise: Educator
My parents are from the South. Both parents were sharecroppers and they had lots of respect for the view of White people, meaning that they thought what the White children had would be the best for me also. So, we were bused to Montezuma Elementary School. There were about ten other Black children. The teacher and classmates were not welcoming. In addition, we had about one and one half hour of travel each way in old buses that broke often on our travels. My parents taught us to respect our teachers so I was quiet about what was really happening to me.

Recommendations/Resolutions/Lessons Learned
The integration of the district should have been both ways. At that time, there weren't late buses; therefore, no after school activities were available.

Testimony #14
Title/Area of Expertise: Software Engineer
My school age (7-9 years old) classmate and I interacted very frequently. I protected him from harm from fellow classmates, shared food, and played sports. When the time came to actually move around and visit each other, I went to his house about two blocks from my apartment complex. The neighborhood was mostly comprised of Irish, Polish, and Italians. But being a fearless youth, I would travel around the neighborhood to yells of "nigger, go back to Africa" all the time.

When I reached the house of my friend, he told me his mom said Black people can't come into their house. It is unbelievable that this 1970s "Karen" would callously raise a child with this chilling message of hate and confusion. I continued demanding for social change from then to now. This was the era of busing of Black students. A look at the affects placed on students bused to this White enclave in bus loads should have been studied before putting the program in place.

Recommendations/Resolutions/Lessons Learned
The very same person who called me the N-word changed her way of thinking. The last time I saw her, I was home one summer on break from college. She was actually happy to see me. We had a long conversation about how life was treating us. It was truly a learning moment, about the nature of many of the people of America. I should have had my mother discuss the incident with my friend's mom. I should have told the school administrators.

Testimony #15
Title/Area of Expertise: Educator
Due to the subtle and blatant racism that I had to face on a daily basis, I quit my job and dealt with the health issues caused from that daily fight.

Recommendations/Resolutions/Lessons Learned
The county superintendent should have intervened to help educate the community and address racism. Walk in other people's shoes and do no harm.

Testimony #16
Title/Area of Expertise: Educator
As a vice principal in San Diego, I was told by my immediate supervisor that she works as hard as a "nigga." When I reported this incident to the district, I was told to get along or else. I left the district seeking better opportunities.

Recommendations/Resolutions/Lessons Learned
I learned just how pervasive racism was throughout all of San Diego County School Districts and had to learn to carefully and proactively pick where I decided to work and be more skillful determining who to trust. Participate in racial human relations training. Engage in self-assessments regarding personal racial biases and how it negatively impacts students, colleagues, and society.

Testimony #17
Title/Area of Expertise: Investor Delivery/Mortgage
When I was in high school, the 2008 presidential election was happening and my school decided to have a mock election. There were very few Black kids at the school and one day during the passing period, this one White boy decided to single me out in the hall and yell, "NOBAMA!" I did not know this boy personally but he decided to yell that at me specifically, probably because I was the only Black kid in the vicinity. I later found out from some of the other Black kids at school that this boy had some racist tendencies. I didn't really deal with it. I was being pushed along by the crowd of students so I didn't have a response. I also think I was so shocked that it happened so randomly. The only thing I did was tell my friends.

Recommendations/Resolutions/Lessons Learned
I think he should have been confronted and questioned as to why he would yell that to a stranger for no reason. By not addressing it, it just allows the behavior to continue.

Ask yourself some internal questions as to why you believe your comments and statements aren't offensive and educate yourself on the experiences of people of a different race. A lot of people think their comments are fine because they are only thinking from their own perspective and their lived experiences instead of someone else's. For someone who is perceived as racist and or makes racist comments I would tell them to seek therapy. A well-informed therapist can help the individual get to the root of why they make racial statements. A good therapist can also assist that individual in exploring what it is about the person(s) they are racially targeting that triggers them. Lastly, I would implore them to examine any implicit bias they have and evaluate how that informs what they say and do when faced with a specific body of people.

Lastly, I would also recommend they read the book *White Fragility: Why It's So Hard for White People to Talk about Racism* by Robin Di Angelo.

Recommendations for ways in which hurtful actions can be alleviated:
1. Repeat what they said aloud, listen to the words, and thereafter place themselves in the receiver's shoes to see how it feels to them when uttered.

2. Before they begin speaking, they should filter their thoughts using the THINK method (*is what I am saying TRUE, is it HELPFUL, is it INSPIRING, is it NECESSARY and is it KIND*) if the answer is no to any of those statements the said individual is to reframe their thought so the answer is yes to all of the above. If they are unable to do so after filtering their thoughts then it is best to keep silent.

Testimony #18
Title/Area of Expertise: Assistant Principal
After four years of being the primary assistant principal/school leader of a high school and the selected choice of the faculty and staff to take over the principal position at the school site. I was also voted to be the principal by the faculty and staff that were on the interview panel. A White male candidate from another school site was selected for the position. In response to the decision, I transferred to another school site.

Recommendations/Resolutions/Lessons Learned
As Black men in America, we have learned that you have to educate yourself first in order to help others. Despite racist behavior directed towards you, be prepared to fight for your human rights, be it physically and/or legally.

Testimony #19
Title/Area of Expertise: Administrative Services Manager
My son was in middle school playing with his friends who are White and they were taking apart a mechanical pencil. My son had a baggie with rubber bands in it (he had braces at the time). A yard duty teacher approached the group of kids and proceeded to ask my son to empty out his pockets. She saw the baggie and said, "Are you selling drugs?" My son told her, "No, these are rubber bands and I don't do drugs." She never questioned nor did she have the White children empty out their pockets.

Recommendations/Resolutions/Lessons Learned
My husband and I met with the principal who stated it was a misunderstanding and the yard duty teacher was new. She was informed that the action was unacceptable and that our son was targeted because he is Black. No other child in the group (a total of 5) was targeted. I demanded a verbal and written apology to my son. I also requested written documentation of this incident and to ensure that his school file was accurate regarding the matter - I was concerned that they may document a negative scenario.

I also recommended more training in the areas of diversity, inclusion, and equity along with sensitivity training.

Testimony #20
Title/Area of Expertise: Retired Educator
I remember in 1973, I was teaching first grade in a small school district in Tucson, AZ. I was just one of two African American teachers in the school district. One day after the school day started, the principal walked a potentially new student and her father to my classroom. I met the potential White student, her White father, and White principal at the door excited to try to make this new student comfortable in this new setting. I also wanted to ensure the father that he was leaving his child with a competent

and caring educator. As the father walked in the door, he looked at me and yelled out, "I will not put my daughter in a nigga's class. She's gotta have another teacher." Of course, I was stunned trying to get a grip of my emotions and try to figure out what had just happened to me. I hadn't been called a nigga since my younger days of growing up in segregated Richmond, VA. My first graders just kept working on their assignment, looking up at the yelling adult in the room. They had no clue as to what the word nigga meant. I cried when I got an opportunity to be alone to reflect on what had just happened. My feelings were hurt. I am a decent human being that was trying to become an excellent teacher. The principal later that day shared with me that she escorted the White father and his White daughter out of the door and told him that it was me as her teacher or no one at her school. I felt good about the support that I received from her but did not get an apology. I did not share this experience with my colleagues.

Recommendations/Resolutions/Lessons Learned
When the principal told me of the resolution of not assigning another teacher to the student and escorting them out of the school, it would have been a golden opportunity for the principal to initiate some sensitive training for the school staff. It would have been beneficial for me to share with the staff what had happened. A conversation on what it feels like to be the only African American teacher on a staff of approximately 30 teachers would benefit us all. The sensitivity training would have provided the staff with skills on how to interact positively with the students of color in their classrooms. Many of the students in the school were Hispanic. I also wish that the principal had reported the incident to the superintendent so that when the father went to enroll his daughter in another school in the district that his application would not be accepted. His daughter's application of enrollment would only be accepted for the school where he resides.

Testimony #21
Title/Area of Expertise: Commercial Real Estate Development
In the scenario where I was questioned as to whether or not my college was accredited, I answered affirmatively, stated the approximate number of students enrolled at the University, the length of the University's existence, and the different majors offered at the University. I have met White people who have never heard of Morgan State University. Since that experience, I typically respond to the question of where I went to

undergrad by saying, "I went to Morgan State University in Baltimore, MD." In cases where I feel that I am being questioned as to whether I went to any type of college at all, my response is "Where did I go to college for which degree?" since I have a BS in Finance, an MBA, and JD.

Recommendations/Resolutions/Lessons Learned
Unfortunately, the learning moment for me has been to answer a simple question like naming a school, and add additional facts into the answer such as the city where it was located or other facts that were not asked in order to avoid an uncomfortable moment similar to the one when I was asked if my college was accredited. Instead of asking me if my school was accredited the interviewer could have said, "I am not that familiar with all of the schools on the East Coast" or "I can't remember which state that is in, where is that again?" or something similar. I am proud of the way that I remained calm and stood up for my school without showing that I felt insulted. Having never heard of Morgan State University should not automatically mean that the school has no education accreditation.

Testimony #22
Title/Area of Expertise: Associate Superintendent
When I was an elementary school student, the high school students would cross our campus as they walked home. One day, one of the White female students spoke to me as she walked across our activities field and said what I thought was, "Hi there baby." One of my best friends at school during that time was a White boy named Jimmy Bees. He looked at me and said why are you smiling after what she said to you?? I looked at him and said, "She called me baby!" He angrily corrected me and said she called you "tar baby!" I was embarrassed and sad after he clarified. So, the next day when she walked through again she yelled, "Hey, tar Baby!" But this time we were armed and ready with rocks we'd collected. Me and my White buddy rocked her off our field. She never crossed our field again. Her behavior was blatantly hateful and racist!! I couldn't comprehend why she would go out of her way to demean me.... I didn't do anything to her to warrant that interaction.

Recommendations/Resolutions/Lessons Learned
I've always taught my daughter to correct folks with love and accept their apology if one is given when they misstep regarding racially insensitive actions or words. If they continue to behave that way, cut them loose. They aren't your friends. With kindness and correction! It's an opportunity to

educate the misinformed. Ask questions before assuming and be willing to listen deeply without feeling like you need to respond or be defensive.

Testimony #23
Title/Area of Expertise: Correctional Administrator-Retired
When I was 6 years old, we moved from Los Angeles, CA, to Sacramento. We first lived in a multicultural community with low income Hispanics, Whites, and low- to middle-income African Americans. Soon after we arrived, I went across the street to attempt to play with a little White boy who was younger than me. As I was approaching his house, he started yelling "nigger." My mother came to our front door and yelled at his mother and said, "She does not know what that is." I asked my mother, was that a bad name for girls? She told me to ignore him and not go to their house. Two years later, we moved to a middle-class neighborhood that was predominately White. I started the fourth grade at Harness Elementary School, and my teacher was an older White woman. I was the only African American in the class. This teacher would not call on me to read out loud in class. Once, my friend asked her why she would not allow me to read. She responded in front of the class that I did not read well enough. She berated me often and showed no patience when I approached her. When my mother went to the school to speak with the principal about her concerns, his response was, "Doesn't she watch TV, doesn't she know she is Negro?" At the time, I did not know why I was being mistreated by her. I learned that years later. I heard, but, do not know for sure, that the teacher's daughter had a negative sexual encounter with an African American male and that is why she had a problem with African Americans. For years, I had low self-esteem issues regarding my academic abilities. I had to work hard to prove myself.

Recommendations/Resolutions/Lessons Learned
The learning moments came years later when I realized she had the issues, not me. In the 1960s, this issue would not be dealt with like today. You need to confront it and tell them.

Testimony #24
Title/Area of Expertise: College Student
In one of my classes in middle school, the teacher had us form groups to work on an assignment. When I went up to a group of students to ask to

join their group, one of the boys thought he was being funny and said, "We don't let niggers in our group." At the time, I had never been called that so I was speechless. I went to the bathroom to cry and then when I returned to class, I worked alone to complete the assignment.

Recommendations/Resolutions/Lessons Learned
I told my mom about the incident. She then instructed me to approach the boy who made the remark and inform him of how rude, racist, and hurtful the comment was. My mom also told me to tell the boy to never speak to me again. The following day in class, the boy apologized. I believe I should have told my principal so that the student could experience some sort of punishment and I think the school should have, in an age appropriate way, educated its students more on Black history and why that word is incredibly inappropriate.

Testimony #25
Title/Area of Expertise: Elementary School Administrator (Retired)
To this day, this experience comes to mind as a teenager in 1956. Riding the bus from a football game, my friend and I were engaged in a conversation, not paying attention to the folks who were getting on or off the bus. During that time, in the segregated South, Blacks sat in the back and Whites in the front. All of a sudden, the bus driver stops the bus and directs his attention to us. Why? Because two White women were sitting behind us. He said, "If you don't get up and move, I will have to call the police." We complied. This was the most humiliating experience of my teenage life. Why did I comply? First and foremost, I thought of my mother, a single parent with very little money. Secondly, I did not want to make matters worse by causing a scene. I must say the students on the bus came to our aid, by saying how they were tired of segregation. It was a very tense moment for everyone on the bus, the bus driver, and the White folks. They did not know what would occur next. Students did not hold back their feelings in a raucous hand clapping way.

Recommendations/Resolutions/Lessons Learned
No resolution. Just a terrible memory that has stayed with me till this day. The shock of the moment could not have been resolved that night. I think we must have these uncomfortable, honest conversations about race and deal with comments head on.

Testimony #26

Title/Area of Expertise: Retired Educator

Growing up in the South, one frequently experienced racist behavior. One of my most impactful and lasting experiences occurred shortly after school integration. I was moved from a warm, supportive, and caring educational environment into a hostile school environment. Upon arrival at the new school, I found that all of my courses were non-academic. I did not have one college preparation course. I asked the counselor why I was not enrolled in college preparation courses. She informed me that I was not college bound. I indicated that I was enrolled in college preparation courses prior to this school change. She said that would not be the case at this new school. So, I informed my mother. We met with the counselor and principal regarding this matter. They, once again, said I was not college material. While my mother did not truly understand what was needed, she insisted that I be placed into correct courses. They finally allowed the change. I found one African American female and one male. The three of us not only completed high school, but continued on to college, completing undergraduate, graduate, and doctoral studies.

Recommendations/Resolutions/Lessons Learned

Yes, with our aggressive action, we were able to positively influence my educational pathway and career trajectory. I am a life-long counselor and serve as a role model to many of my family members and friends.

For both experiences, whether the career mobility challenges or the misadvising regarding college preparation, I believe the negative perceptions of African American attainment was and continues to be pervasive. For the high school counselor, she made the assumption that Black children were not able to handle college preparation coursework.

The appropriate thing to do would have been to talk with each student to identify educational goals or review the academic records from the previous school to assess each student's background. Both behaviors were unacceptable. Therefore, parental involvement is critical for children and identifying a supportive mentor is imperative. I think that it would have been difficult to confront such an individual at the time of these incidents. However, at this stage, I would have called attention to the racist behavior. If it was a colleague, I would have alerted the individual to the action and talked about more effective ways to address the issue. I would recommend appropriate workshops and relevant materials designed to educate that individual. Also, I would recommend training and materials that address microaggression.

Testimony #27
Title/Area of Expertise: Retired Child Care Provider
I had never been a part of any government group or Black Student Union group before attending UCI. In the years 1978-79, I became a member of the Black Steering Committee at UCI. This is when I was first introduced to the struggles of minority groups on campus having to fight one another to get a bigger piece of the money pie to support the needs of our group organizations. I learned that the so-called "majority" was always awarded the biggest slice. Really, this was preparing us for real life. Minority groups would have tension among each other during that time. We needed more funding and we were not going to get it from the majority.

Recommendations/Resolutions/Lessons Learned
We realized we could not keep allowing ourselves to fight against one another. After all, we were in the same boat. We were all given a little of nothing for the whole year. We worked out our differences with one another. Then we began to work out new strategies to obtain the much needed funds we would need for the entire year. I believe that this was the best way to go, with the situation at hand. To me, society is set up to keep minorities fighting and speaking against one another. It begins the moment school age children are taught to think they are superior to others because of their skin color, riches, or the influential status of their parents.

We must teach the children at an early age to respect themselves and others. This is difficult because there are so many people teaching their children to hate others just for being different. We have to teach our children to know their worth and to know they are equal to anyone and they can be anything they desire to be.

Testimony #28
Title/Area of Expertise: CEO
A little over three years ago, my son was told by a fellow student to "Shut up slave" while in 4th grade. My son handled it beautifully by repeating history and telling the other student about the abolition of slavery and that he would not be talked to that way. The student then said, "Well, I'm American," to which my son replied, "I am too." I did go to the principal's office but, more importantly, I praised my son for the way he confronted the situation with dignity.

Recommendations/Resolutions/Lessons Learned
We chose not to talk to the other family but dealt with it within our own family. We continued to praise our son and let him know that education is the best defense. I would have preferred to sit down and talk with the other family but I did not have confidence it would do any good. In fact, I thought it would escalate the situation because I was so angry. Looking back, I wish I had insisted on meeting with the other family.
Educate yourself. Put yourself in different environments so you can broaden your perspective.

Testimony #29
Title/Area of Expertise: Retired Teacher (Reading Specialist)/Former Business Owner/Entrepreneur
Refused service and use of restroom facilities in segregated South and parts of Indiana during early childhood and young adulthood. Taught to accept it and walk away for your own safety. Feelings of anger, frustration, violation.

Recommendations/Resolutions/Lessons Learned
The only resolution was to walk away, head held high. At the time, it was handled correctly because it could have resulted in loss of my life. Speak up, call it like you see it. Boldly make it known that you will not tolerate or accept biased, racist treatment. Not sure how to avoid ignorance and racism.

Testimony #30
Title/Area of Expertise: Division Counsel/Corporate Attorney
While a sophomore at UCI, a group of my friends (6 Black females) went to visit another friend who lived in a nearby apartment complex with a large pool. We decided to put on our swimsuits and get into the pool, but as soon as we entered the pool, a group of White swimmers got out. They then went up to the second floor of the complex and threw soap down into the pool, yelling at us to "wash the Black off."

Recommendations/Resolutions/Lessons Learned
We were shaken but tried to stay in the pool for a while (just to show them that they couldn't run us off), but our good time was ruined and we left soon thereafter.

Testimony #31
Title/Area of Expertise: Division Counsel/Corporate Attorney
While a senior at UCI, one evening I drove a friend of mine (a Black male) home to the apartment he shared with other students in Newport Beach. While traveling down a dark stretch of Jamboree Highway south of PCH, we were pulled over for "driving while Black." The officer shone a bright light in the car so that we could not see, took both of our licenses, and questioned why we were out at night. We told him that we were UCI students and I was just giving my friend a ride home. He said he didn't believe us, because Black people didn't live in Newport Beach, and pointed to my friend's license, which showed his permanent address in Oakland, as evidence that we were lying. He then said he was going to call in my license plate to see if my car was stolen. He told us to keep our hands up on the dash as he went to his cruiser to run the license plate. I heard the police radio come back a few minutes later saying the car was registered to my parents (as I told him) at the address on my driver's license. However, he made us sit there 45 minutes after my story was verified. I remember trying to calm down my male passenger, who was ready to get out and confront the officer. I was afraid, even back then, that we would be beaten or shot.

Recommendations/Resolutions/Lessons Learned
After about an hour of holding us for no purpose, he gave us our licenses and allowed us to leave but he followed me all the way to Newport Beach until I dropped my friend off.

Testimony #32
Title/Area of Expertise: Division Counsel/Corporate Attorney
While working at a notable Wall Street law firm, an influential large client in Texas informed the firm that they did not want me working on their case.

Recommendations/Resolutions/Lessons Learned
To their credit, my law firm turned down their business.

Testimony #33
Title/Area of Expertise: Division Counsel/Corporate Attorney
While at a hearing for a case in Tallahassee, Florida, I decided to take a walk after court one day. While walking down the street enjoying the

spring day, a car [drove] by, threw something at me, and called me the N-word.

Recommendations/Resolutions/Lessons Learned
Shaken, I turned around, went back to the hotel, and didn't mention the incident to my co-workers or anyone else.

Testimony #34
Title/Area of Expertise: Division Counsel/Corporate Attorney
When considering a possible promotion and move to our corporate headquarters in Louisville, Kentucky, while at a corporate attorney retreat, one of the Louisville attorneys started giving me unsolicited advice on the best places to live and said I should move to a certain neighborhood because they had a private school system and none of "those kids" goes there.

Recommendations/Resolutions/Lessons Learned
I politely asked him what he meant and then informed him that I was the mother of one of "those kids" and knew that I could never move to Louisville.

Testimony #35
Title/Area of Expertise: Division Counsel/Corporate Attorney
Early on in my 25+ year career at the Fortune 500 company I retired from, one of the Vice-Presidents at my company (a White male) didn't want to work with me, despite the fact that I was the only in-house attorney with the relevant background and training for his situation. He asked if he could get one of the "male" attorneys to work with him. I informed him that I was the only attorney with the knowledge he needed, but that he could go find another attorney if he wanted to because I had other work to do. I informed my supervisor (the company's General Counsel) what happened and returned to my desk.

Recommendations/Resolutions/Lessons Learned
Happy ending here; this same Vice President eventually began to seek out my expertise and we became friends. He was one of my staunchest supporters at the company.

Testimony #36
Title/Area of Expertise: Division Counsel/Corporate Attorney
While shopping in the salon shoe section of the flagship Bloomingdale's store in NYC, I bought several pairs of shoes (I have a thing for shoes). When I was heading to the escalator with my bags after making my purchases, I was stopped by the security guard and asked to empty out my bags because a White woman said she put her purse down and it was just stolen. Of course, I was the only Black shopper in sight and no one else was stopped or questioned.

Recommendations/Resolutions/Lessons Learned
I furiously complied, just to show them that I wasn't a thief, and dumped the contents of my bags onto the floor in front of the escalator. Then I marched back to the register and returned all the shoes.

Testimony #37
Title/Area of Expertise: Division Counsel/Corporate Attorney
My son was told at four years old, by another preschooler, that "Black kids don't belong at this school." He came home to ask why the little boy said that to him since his skin was brown (4-year-olds are very literal). I went up to the preschool the next day and reported the incident, reminded the preschool that they had an obligation to protect my child from intimidation and harassment, and asked to meet with the boy's parents.

The school arranged a meeting, where the parents protested that they didn't know where their little boy got that racist idea. I told them he was too young to come up with it by himself, and he had to learn that type of hate from home. I also threatened publicity and legal action if it happened again.

Recommendations/Resolutions/Lessons Learned
The parents ended up withdrawing their son from the school.

Testimony #38
Title/Area of Expertise: Division Counsel/Corporate Attorney
When my son was in high school, an Asian student called him the N-word. I went up to the school, demanded a meeting with the parents, and was told by way of explanation that their son was under a great deal of stress.

Recommendations/Resolutions/Lessons Learned
The school said they filed a police report (I asked for a copy but was told I couldn't have one since the boy's name was mentioned) and again I threatened publicity and legal action if nothing was done.

Testimony #39
Title/Area of Expertise: Journeyman Machinist/Builder
While traveling through the South by bus with my 3-year-old nephew, I was called out of my name and refused use of the gas station bathroom. The bus air conditioning had stopped working and he got sick. I will spare you and not be more graphic, but it was bad and required a change of clothes.

Recommendations/Resolutions/Lessons Learned
The resolution? Treat us with dignity! We have a sick 3-year-old human being here! If I decided to take the time, because I thought it might be helpful, I would steer them toward learning more actual American history, rather than the typical whitewashed version in order to learn more about White privilege, White supremacy, and the history of people of color in this world.

Testimony #40
Title/Area of Expertise: Community Economic Development
My oldest son attended San Diego High School and during a meeting with his White counselor, he said to my son, "You are a big dog and you know where big dogs end up–in the dog pound." Being a mother of four sons, I taught them how to listen to what is being said about them and not react. The message was clear–you are a Black man and Black men end up in prison. What I noticed is that my two light-skinned sons were heavily impacted by racism. It was the educational system that was used to impact them negatively.

Recommendations/Resolutions/Lessons Learned
This was an extremely important learning moment because my son is a big man and this counselor was encouraging him to live a life not made for him. He was stereotyped and not given adequate assistance from a school that should have been encouraging his education. It could have been resolved by taking this matter to his superiors/school principal and

following the right chain of command if necessary. Instead of reacting immediately, hear and heed yourself.

Testimony #41
Title/Area of Expertise: Community Engagement Aide/Public Health
When I was 16, I was a member of an ambassador program and was planning to travel to Europe for two weeks. One of the group leaders already gave me the feeling that she thought I didn't belong in the group nor deserved to go on the trip. As a minor, it is required to have the signature of both parents in order to get a passport and leave the country. My mother had been the only parent taking me to the pre-trip meetings. When the leaders said we needed the signatures of both parents, she specifically came up to me and asked if I would have a problem getting both signatures. I asked her why she thought I would have a problem getting both signatures and she just got red in the face and never answered my question. I told my mom what she said and then my father came to the following meetings. There were further instances while on the trip that I told my mother about and when I came back, my parents and I wrote a letter to the organization, detailing my experience with the given group leader, letting them know of her unfitness to travel with youth ambassador groups anymore and they fired her.

Recommendations/Resolutions/Lessons Learned
I dealt with a previous incident by calling her out in front of my cohort, stating that I would pass my comprehensive and I would be going abroad. I later learned that when I received a department award, she told the story of our interactions completely different from what actually happened. I recommend documenting each incidence and if it can be addressed at that time, address it then, diplomatically.

Testimony #42
Title/Area of Expertise: Social Work; Special Education
The incident occurred during my second year of school when I was a dorm advisor. Being a dorm advisor, I lived on campus in one of the dorms and my boyfriend at the time came to visit me. We were sitting in the car parked behind the dorms where most of the dorm advisors were able to park. We noticed a car drive up behind us and put their high beams on. We found out that they were campus security as they approached the car. We

were told to get out of the car and we tried to explain who we were; however, we were ignored and told to face the car and put our hands on the hood. I was like, "what for?" and was yelled at, telling me to turn around and place my hands on the hood. I kept thinking, what is going on and why is this happening? They ended up searching my boyfriend first. Then they ended up searching me. There was not a female officer around, but two males. This may not sound right, but they did not do anything out of the ordinary. But, I did feel very violated. I was so ashamed that I didn't tell anyone, not even my supervisors or mentor at the campus. I knew in my heart that if we were two White students, that we would not have been searched the way we were. I was attending a campus where less than 2% of the campus was Black students.

Recommendations/Resolutions/Lessons Learned
I never reported this incident to anyone. I learned that I needed to be more careful about what I do, where I go, and how I conduct myself. I am a Navy brat and grew up in several different cities, with my last actual city I grew up in to be very diverse due to it being surrounded by a Marine base. I grew up around people of various cultures and did not experience any instances of blatant racism prior to this. My eyes were opened to what my father had been trying to teach me when I was young.

Testimony #43
Title/Area of Expertise: Social Work; Special Education
While I was still attending the same school, I was a member of a sorority and a few of our Sorors came to town for a party that we were throwing the next night. We had just finished having dinner at the Souplantation and began walking downtown to enjoy the sites and get some fresh air.

We were laughing, talking, and just having a good ole' time. I all of a sudden heard someone say, "N-----r, get out of my way," and we see this older White man on a bike go by us. We all stopped and I felt a little chuckle come out of me. Not that I thought the experience was funny, because it definitely was not. I think I was kinda taken aback as I have never been called that before. I came out of my fog because I heard someone very distraught and crying. I turned around; it was my sorority sister. I went over to console her as all the Sorors were doing and I felt her pain.

Recommendations/Resolutions/Lessons Learned
I think we handled it the best we could at the time. The support and love that was shared as a way to cope and manage with the incident was enough. We could have made a police report, but I am not sure what would have come from it. It was night and we really didn't get a good look at the man.

If I felt safe and thought I wasn't in danger of physical violence, I would try to engage them in a discussion as to why they would say something like that or do whatever behavior they engaged in. Hopefully, I could ask questions and engage the person in a civil discussion in efforts of getting them to question their thinking or behavior. If they are receptive, then hopefully they return to the table for further discussions.

Testimony #44
Title/Area of Expertise: Educator
I am from Milwaukee, Wisconsin. Milwaukee is known to be the most segregated city in the nation. I lived in the North side, which was an area that was saturated by Black residents. My first experience of racism happened during my time as an undergrad. I attended the University of Wisconsin - Madison. The school's population is about 40,000 students; 2% of the population was Black. My first year was during the conclusion of the OJ Simpson trial. When the verdict was announced, I was in my dorm room. I ran throughout the dorm yelling, "The Juice is loose" when the jury found OJ not guilty. After I celebrated, I headed to class. People's reactions were split. All the Black students were giving each other high fives or saying "hell yeah!" while the White students were upset or crying.

My roommate and I had the same calculus class. After class, we hung out with a friend and then headed to the dining hall. After we finished eating, we left the dining hall and headed back to our dorm room. We walked to the door, and our jaws dropped! "Nigger, go back to Africa! Chink, go back to China!" was written on the dry erase board attached to our door. I recognized the handwriting. It belonged to a girl named Erin who lived on our floor and who was in my chemistry lecture lab and laboratory section. I looked at my roommate and said, "It's on!" I ran to my house fellow's room and vigorously knocked on his door. He answered and asked what's wrong. I told him that I was getting kicked out of the dorm tonight and I just wanted to let him know. I then headed to Erin's room. She was already outside of her room.

"So you think you can just write any kind of bullshit on someone's door!?"
"What do you mean?"

"Don't play stupid! Since you want to play games, grab your backpack and come to my door!" My house fellow then asked her if she wrote the racial slurs, and she admitted it. She claimed that she was joking around and didn't think I was going to react this way. She continued to say that she's from a farm north of Madison and that she only has seen Black people on MTV. I jumped in and informed her that all Black people don't sing, rap, and dance. I also told her that if she has the nerve to call me a nigger again, I will show them that I'm no punk and will make sure to give every girl on the wing a reason to cry and run home to their mommy and daddy. From that day forward, when my roommate and I got off the elevator, every girl in the wing would look down. They never gave eye contact or spoke. When I entered the restroom, they hurried out. Midyear, my roommate and I causally discussed the dynamics in our wing. It seemed as though she was blaming me about not being able to develop relationships with the other girls.

I told my roommate that I don't control her. If she wants to speak to them, that's her prerogative; I also told my roommate that I have no desire in befriending anyone who had the need to embarrass, disrespect, and belittle me. Then I questioned her because they did the exact action toward her. That moment caused me to move differently at the university. As time progressed, I found out I wasn't alone; many Black students were sharing their experiences with racism on campus. I continued to encounter racism as a student at UW-Madison, from being profiled and followed in the bookstore to being stopped by the campus police because I fit the description of someone else. I hated my college experience because of the constant harassment and microaggressions.

Recommendations/Resolutions/Lessons Learned
With the dorm situation, yes [there was resolution]. Erin was written up. Learning moments - after my first year, I never went anywhere alone when the sun went down. I felt it was necessary to have someone back me up in case I was being accused of something I didn't do. I also noticed that I wasn't being harassed as much by campus police. I still presently have that mentality. I hate being out at night... especially driving. Sometimes you can have a courageous conversation with racists. Oftentimes, the racists I have encountered are bullies and think they are never wrong.

Because of politics within education, file a uniform complaint so there is official documentation.

Testimony #45
Title/Area of Expertise: Declined to State
As a child, I experienced racism in the first grade while attending Our Lady of Sorrows Catholic School in Chicago, IL. The school was integrated. If your parents can afford to pay, you were accepted. There was work going on and, kids being kids, we were nosy. Plywood had been placed over an area that had been excavated and circular holes were cut in the plywood to allow the workers to put hoses through. Our game was to see who could put their foot in the hole and get it out. Everyone was successful except for one little White girl. She lost her shoe in the hole. She told the nun (we had nuns as teachers) that I "knocked her down, took her shoe off, and threw it in the hole." I told the nun that I didn't do that and the other children told her the same thing. She didn't believe us. We were not White. She called me a "liar" and slapped me. This person, that was supposed to be married to God, slapped and called me a liar because she believed a little White girl's story.

Recommendations/Resolutions/Lessons Learned
As far as the nun slapping me, one of my older sisters visited the school and had a chat with the nun. No more problems.

Testimony #46
Title/Area of Expertise: Declined to State
The first time I was called a "nigger" I was 12 years old. I was in the locker room after gym class in 7th grade (Fairdale High School/Louisville, Kentucky). I was bused there from the mostly Black neighborhood I lived in as part of the federally mandated school integration plan. I remember a few people (I presumed they were parents) standing outside the school with anti-busing signs as the buses rolled in from my neighborhood on my first day of school in 1976. Early on in the first couple of weeks of class, I was at my locker in gym class getting dressed. A much bigger White kid, still in his t-shirt and gym shorts, came over to where I was standing, punched me, and shoved me to the floor, calling me a nigger in the process.

Recommendations/Resolutions/Lessons Learned
The reason I remember it so vividly to this day is that I remember staring up at the kid's face while he stood over me. I can still see the silhouettes of the other kids in the background in the distance. I remember being startled in the moment and at how angry he was and wondering why. The other kids, mostly White, looked on with some of them laughing. None of them said anything or did anything to help. After a moment, I gathered myself, stood up, and finished dressing, and eventually went to the next class. I never told anyone about it to this day.

Testimony #47
Title/Area of Expertise: Attorney
In my senior year of high school, despite taking honors courses with excellent grades (where often I was one of only a handful of Black students in the class), the college/career counselor did not talk to me about college or encourage me to sign up to take the PSAT. Instead, she told me that with my typing and shorthand skills I would make an excellent secretary. I ended up applying late to take the PSAT, only because my mother was aware of its importance (my older brother graduated from the U.S. Air Force Academy) and she came up to the school and raised hell. I ended up scoring extremely high on the PSAT (and later on the SAT) and ultimately was recruited and admitted to every college I applied to. When I graduated, the high school tried to deny giving me the gold seal and cord that I had earned with my grades, saying that I had not attended the California Scholastic Federation club meetings (which no one told me about).

Recommendations/Resolutions/Lessons Learned
My mother, who had served as President of the PTA and was well known at the school, came to my defense and I eventually received the honors I deserved.

Testimony #48
Title/Area of Expertise: Retired
I was in college and the KKK came on campus but I didn't know who they were because I wasn't familiar with them. Everyone was screaming and saying, "The KKK are on Battle Street" which ran through campus "so

you better run." Even the people downtown were nice to us because they knew we would spend money at their businesses.

Recommendations/Resolutions/Lessons Learned
None provided.

Testimony #49
Title/Area of Expertise: Retired
I wanted to be an airline stewardess when I came out of college but was not able to apply because of segregation. Then I decided to pursue my graduate degree. Southern did not have a master's program and LSU was segregated. However, since it was separate but equal, the State of Louisiana paid for me to go to UC Berkeley for my graduate degree.

Recommendations/Resolutions/Lessons Learned
None provided.

Healthcare

Testimony #1
Title/Area of Expertise: Registered Nurse
On my first day of work and orientation, I informed the Director of Nursing that I was not planning on working 12-hour shifts in their Intensive Care Unit or sleeping on a cot, while my roommate had a double bed. In addition, I needed a key to the front door because under my teachings the back door was no longer in existence in 1980.

Recommendations/Resolutions/Lessons Learned
Before the end of my first shift that same day, I was delivered a key to the front door. When I got off work that evening there was a furniture company moving double beds into all of the apartments in the nursing complex. I was not fearful of using my voice to speak up for my rights. Inform others up front what you are experiencing and that it is not right. Give them examples of comments or actions that might make them aware of the situation.

Testimony #2
Title/Area of Expertise: Physician
My first experience with blatant racism occurred during my early childhood growing up in the state of Mississippi. I remember clearly the

evening my mother became acutely ill, when suddenly she went into a coughing spell and, with concern for it not getting better, was taken to the local designated "colored" hospital. Upon arrival at the emergency room, she was checked in by the nurse, but was told she would have to wait to be seen because the doctor was on a break. After a period of time and not receiving any update on her progress, the nurse frantically comes out of the room, saying, "I am so sorry, but your mother is gone." It is a fact that access to healthcare in Mississippi in the 60s was as grim then as it is today, ranking last, or close to last, in almost every leading health outcome. Coupled with systematic discrimination, Blacks in our community did not routinely seek preventative care and/or regular checkups, and there were only a few medical professionals of color to identify with the issues we faced. I would later learn that my mother's death was a result of cardiac complications associated with an easily treatable thyroid condition called Graves' disease. But at that time, the issue that resonated with me was why did she have to wait so long in an urgent care setting in that "colored" hospital and the audacity of an ER physician to be on break and not taking care of patients. During one of the most critical times of a child's development, the nurturing presence of a mother was taken away, leaving in the wake emptiness devoid of comfort and assurance. It was at this very moment that I became convinced that I would become a doctor so no child would have to experience this feeling.

Recommendations/Resolutions/Lessons Learned
As healthcare providers, we continue to see the disparity in healthcare outcomes in our underserved communities. The reasons are multifactorial to include limited access to quality and affordable healthcare, poorly addressed social determinants such as food insecurity, healthy lifestyle choices, and education on disease states that disproportionately affect people of color. The root of this particular issue, and how it can be addressed, is through change of our healthcare delivery systems. There must be action to hold insurance companies, hospitals, and physician reimbursement systems accountable for providing quality of care versus volume of care.

Testimony #3
Title/Area of Expertise: Educator & Activist
On April 26, 2019, I lost my 29-year-old big brother due to what I believe was blatant SYSTEMIC racism. Shawn Edward Washington II died in an

Emergency Room after sitting for eight hours while his lungs actively filled with blood. Shawn couldn't breathe and expressed it multiple times, yet his healthcare team was more concerned with the color of his skin and health insurance status. Shawn was asked multiple times about having AIDS and/or being on drugs (neither of which were true) all while he was struggling to obtain air. I watched my big brother, best friend, and hero have his life stripped from him by the very system designed to save our lives! Our medical systems unfortunately have been doing this for hundreds of years to African Americans and getting away with it. Shawn never got a chance to meet his now 11-month-old daughter, not due to gun violence, police brutality, drugs, or drunk drivers. Shawn Edward Washington II lost his life to a health care system that is lacking empathy, compassion, understanding, and love for the African American community.

Recommendations/Resolutions/Lessons Learned
The biggest learning moment was a profound understanding of the huge disparities within healthcare and the need for change.

Testimony #4
Title/Area of Expertise: Computers
I've been kicked out of Kaiser Emergency at least two times. I used to have chronic back pain. I went to Kaiser Emergency in Manteca. The White doctor came out and immediately said, "I don't have any narcotics to give you." I asked him why he would say that. I hadn't even been through triage yet, and not once did I say I was there for narcotics. They ended up calling the cops on me because I was in pain and wanted proper care.

Recommendations/Resolutions/Lessons Learned
No resolution. My learning moment was that Kaiser didn't care. I reported it to member services and they did nothing. I should not have been treated like that. I'm a member of Kaiser.

Testimony #5
Title/Area of Expertise: Hospital Assistant
After getting off work, I stopped by the store, still in my professional work attire. My granddaughter and I were walking down the aisle in the grocery

store when an elder White woman saw us coming down the aisle and immediately grabbed her purse and acted abruptly, scattering to get into the refrigerated doors to get her items while keeping one eye on us. My granddaughter and I just continued walking and talking. I looked at my granddaughter and asked her did she just notice anything different? She replied, "Yes, that lady thought that we were going to grab her purse, because she reached for it and held onto it as we were passing."

Recommendations/Resolutions/Lessons Learned
There was no resolution, but definitely a learning moment for my 11-year-old granddaughter as she recognized an example of classic stereotype racism. There was really no sure way to deal with it, unless I approached her, which could have turned into a disaster. I did speak out in passing loud enough for her to hear explaining to my granddaughter what had just happened and how her behavior was not acceptable. To avoid any confrontation and since we do have freedom of speech, I would just speak out so that our voices can be heard and not just ignored. Black Lives Matter!

Testimony #6
Title/Area of Expertise: Registered Nurse
While at work, I had a female patient who was approximately 64 years old. She suffered from chronic pain. The nurse who cared for her on the earlier shift told me that she would always give medication 15 minutes before [the evening news] due to her unbearable pain. When I arrived with her pain meds before bed, she told me she didn't trust me to give her the right meds because "the Black ones never give her the right meds." I told her that I had the meds that the doctor ordered and I let her read the packet herself. She still wanted "another" nurse to give her pain meds even if she would have to wait longer. The break nurse gave her the pain meds an hour and a half later. She didn't complain again that night.

Recommendations/Resolutions/Lessons Learned
Some people test you to see if you are as good as your word. I learned to under-promise and over-deliver with those types of people. I believe the way it was handled was the best way. Everyone has a right to receive the best patient-centered care available. By morning, this patient found that she had received just that. I would suggest that they give each individual the benefit of the doubt. Don't condemn an entire race based on

their previous interactions or preconceived notions. Then, I would smile kindly and leave.

Judicial/Law

Testimony #1
Title/Area of Expertise: Judge
As a relatively new attorney, I worked for a governmental institution. I was one of two Black people in the office of close to 100. There was a training program that went by seniority. When my time arrived, a junior attorney was sent to the program. When confronted, the head of the office explained it was his prerogative to send whom he pleased. Up until that point, the program was based on seniority. To my knowledge, afterwards, it went back to being based on seniority.

Recommendations/Resolutions/Lessons Learned
I was devastated but waited patiently. I was sent after a junior person. I learned as much as possible, which made me more marketable. After completing the 6-month program, I left the office for a much better paying position. They meant it for evil, but God meant it for good.

Testimony #2
Title/Area of Expertise: Judge
I was the first Black person at the firm. I excelled and was told I would be the first woman partner. My supervising partner had an affair with a White woman with marginal legal skills. She became the first woman partner and I was asked to wait.

Recommendations/Resolutions/Lessons Learned
I left for a much better paying job. Again, they meant it for evil, but God meant it for good.

Testimony #3
Title/Area of Expertise: Judge
As a judge, having paid the requisite dues, I asked to be assigned in a division that is considered relatively elite and had never had a Black [presiding judge].

I was passed over twice and did not get the position until I cut a deal with an ambitious White woman.

Recommendations/Resolutions/Lessons Learned
I've learned the higher up you go, the more insidious the racism. I also learned to be patient and trust God. The first two experiences, and there are many more, the racism forced me to look for another job. Each time, I found a better job with more room for advancement and more pay. In all of my professional experiences with racism, I was the only Black person or the highest-ranking Black person.

There was no one to assist me. And, in those professional settings, you have to be very careful how you handle matters or you will be labeled and have difficulty advancing in the profession. It is clearly an old boys club and the old boys are firmly in control. *How to Be an Antiracist* [by Ibram X. Kendi] should be required reading. Implicit bias training is not enough. Whether the racist comments/behavior is intentional or not, the results are the same.

Life Experiences

Testimony #1
Title/Area of Expertise: Retired Community College Dean
In high school, I joined Y-Teens–not at my school but in a citywide club of other African American teens. The school club was for Whites only.

Recommendations/Resolutions/Lessons Learned
I made good friendships with African American teens. A few years later, the YWCA integrated and my mother served on the Board. Years later, my aunt became the first African American to serve as National President. The true satisfaction was when I discovered that I had more fun with the Y-Teens for Blacks and that I didn't want to live in the same community where I taught school. It was way more fun to live in Detroit with Black roommates socializing with other Blacks.

We need to have extra strong conversations–letting the other person know that what they said or did was hurtful to you and explain why–not just express your hurt or blame them. We need to try to have the "other" person know our feelings and how they would feel if that happened to them.

Testimony #2
Title/Area of Expertise: Educator/Middle School
Five years ago, my husband and I were looking to purchase a home in an area where the White population is over 80%. We were asked to provide bank statements after looking at a home for the first time. We told the realtor NO and that we wanted to see their bank statements as well.

Recommendations/Resolutions/Lessons Learned
We knew immediately that we did not want to purchase the home. In hindsight, we should have filed a complaint with the Equal Housing Opportunity office. I would recommend getting to know the person that you have racist feelings against. It really becomes a heart thing in how you deal with others. Treating others the way you want to be treated or your family members is key.

Testimony #3
Title/Area of Expertise: Retired Educator
I had to drink from COLORED water fountains. I have several incidents in the south during the fifties and sixties of overt racism. I was at the Selma to Montgomery March as a college student in Montgomery. The first time I was called the N-word was in San Diego at a McDonald's in Mission Valley.

Recommendations/Resolutions/Lessons Learned
I had the manager call the police and then had the racist arrested.

Testimony #4
Title/Area of Expertise: Educator
I was trying to see the Westview HS grad night set up and a White woman stepped in front of me and told me that I could not enter again. When I questioned why, she responded that I had just been in there. She also stated, "I know you've been in there three times before and you can't come back in." I immediately told her that I was a parent and I wanted to see it again. She threw her hands up and immediately began screaming, "Help, she's attacking me, she's attacking me!" The police were called on me.
Recommendations/Resolutions/Lessons Learned
I would have videotaped the entire situation on my phone to show proof that she was the aggressor and not me.

Testimony #5
Title/Area of Expertise: Licensed Psychiatric Technician
My husband, my son (9 years old at the time), and I took a trip to New York. We were browsing a souvenir store when I noticed that two store clerks were trailing me in the store. They were not concerned with my husband and son who were in another part of the store (husband is light-skin Mexican) and they were not concerned with a White family that was browsing. After five minutes of having the store clerks right on top of me, I yelled out, "Why are you following me? I was ready to purchase all of these items. You are not following anyone else in here. Why me?" Both store clerks looked startled but said nothing. I continued to rant and accuse them of profiling me. My husband grabbed my son and ushered me out of the store. I had to explain to my son what happened and why I had an outburst. It was a teachable moment.

Recommendations/Resolutions/Lessons Learned
I believe the resolution to racial profiling is to change the narrative of how African Americans are portrayed on all media platforms. The way African Americans are portrayed in movies, TV, and the news allows stereotypes to be confirmed and flourish.

Testimony #6
Title/Area of Expertise: Pastor
When I was 11 years old, in Concord, California, another 11-year-old White kid pulled a rifle on me, and called me "nigger." I was in shock, but the one kid that stood up for me was another White kid who I was playing with. I ran and told my aunt what happened, and she called the police. The boy was arrested and taken somewhere in the police car with his father in the backseat.

Recommendations/Resolutions/Lessons Learned
No, the kid was not prosecuted, and was sent home from jail the same day. One should think five times before speaking. See the other person as a Human Being.

Testimony #6
Title/Area of Expertise: Educator
Walking down the street two months ago, I was behind a woman for a couple of blocks and about ten minutes. Two people crossed by her in a

car, pointed and said, "Hey there is a Black guy following you, be careful." The woman starts to hold her purse and begins running away from me.

Recommendations/Resolutions/Lessons Learned
I laughed.

Testimony #7
Title/Area of Expertise: Technical Manager
Once at the age of eight, and growing up in a very diverse community of Black, Filipino, Hispanic, Japanese, Vietnamese, and White, I was invited to a new neighbors home, who happened to be Asian, to play. Shortly after arrival, I was told I had to go home. When I asked why, I was told, "My mom says you have to go... it's because you're Black." I was severely hurt because we were having a great time playing together, and the other little girl (non-Black) was allowed to stay.

Recommendations/Resolutions/Lessons Learned
Visibly upset on my way home, my elder sister (13) and I crossed paths. When asked what was wrong, I told her. She was really upset, but reminded me that we were so much better than those people and to never associate with them again. She impressed upon me that our family was great, we owned our home, and we should not associate with people with those attitudes, who were not in our neighborhood, but in an area where people could only rent homes, and weren't truly a part of our permanent community. In that scenario, I had to exit as requested; however, I continued to make friends of all cultures, whose parents didn't hold those negative attitudes. Because of that, I became ever more confident that being Black, being a part of a solid family, being engaged in our community through service, and trying to be the best in areas we could excel in, gave my siblings and me a sense of confidence.

I truly felt like being me...Black, a woman, a Christian, a friend, and setting goals for higher achievement was a blessing. In retrospect, I'd ask them to stop, and think about what they are saying; and ask themselves would they want a similar comment to be said about themselves or a family member? Negative comments can go both ways. I would remind them that 400 plus years of free labor was afforded to this nation on the backs of Black folks; we have every right to be equally treated and afforded mutual respect. I would recommend that every age person in the U.S. watch the Netflix special *13th*.

Testimony #8
Title/Area of Expertise: Network Engineer
I was 20 years old, dating and living with a White woman my age. We had been together a couple years. We were out at a store in her car but I was driving. We got into an argument and she tried to kick me out of her car. I told her no. She then said that she would call the police on me and stated, "When they get here, who do you think they're gonna believe?" I got out of the car and walked home. We broke up shortly after that incident.

Recommendations/Resolutions/Lessons Learned
Learning moments: If you're around someone long enough, you'll find out who they really are. They'll tell you. They'll show you. When someone tells you and shows you who they are, believe them.

Testimony #9
Title/Area of Expertise: Government Relations
A woman once rear-ended my car while I was stopped at a red light. We both pulled into a nearby parking lot to exchange information, or so I thought. She got out of her car and called me a "nigger bitch." Right away, I could tell she was intoxicated - I called the police. They towed her car and I was informed this was not her first DUI.

Recommendations/Resolutions/Lessons Learned
This was a learning moment for me because it was the first time I'd experienced racism from another person of color. It caught me off guard. I'm not sure there was another way to resolve this one. I would advise people to take a deep look at the root of their behavior and/or actions. They may stem from something taught at home with no real self-reflection. I would advise people to look at the humanity of every situation and to see each other as humans deserving respect. Also, the best thing they can do is raise children who do not exhibit similar behavior.

Testimony #10
Title/Area of Expertise: Retired Administrator
When I was in high school, my mother worked for the superintendent of the school district in which I attended school. The superintendent knew I

was having a hard time finding a job so he had me come to the district office and ask for a specific person. I did so and I was given a job copying records on microfiche for the summer. One of the other summer employees, related to the assistant superintendent from out of town, became a person I ate lunch with.

I invited her to my aunt's house for lunch one day and when we got back, her cousin called her. Not knowing she was on a speakerphone, the cousin asked her, "How was it in "nigger town?" She was embarrassed and turned red. I said nothing and went to my location to work. She came to me later and we had a discussion about racism, the N-word, and attitudes.

Recommendations/Resolutions/Lessons Learned
There was no resolution, but it taught me that people aren't always who they claim to be. Also, that people in charge can do what they want to do. If they want to hire you, it doesn't matter what your application says or even if you complete one, they can hire you if they want to do so.

Testimony #11
Title/Area of Expertise: Telecommunications and C.C.T.V
I was once called a ni**** by a lady with her husband next to her. I threw my juice in her face. Because I don't believe in hitting women - I put hands on the husband, "I beat his a**." He didn't attempt to stop her from saying what she said. He also took offense at the juice in her face.

Recommendations/Resolutions/Lessons Learned
I wouldn't say this was a learning moment for me. Hopefully, for them. The situation was handled exactly the way it was dealt with. In that instance, more White people were there, so it's a learning experience for all. I don't feel a real racist will ever stop unless there is a life-changing experience. I think that couple will either think twice or hate us even more.

I have had to discipline a Jewish guy before. All of these racists have one thing in common - ignorance. They say ignorance can only be resolved by education. That's not true. This kind of ignorance has to be taught by pain. When there is a consequence behind your words or action, it will most likely change your view or make you think before you act or say something. I don't believe in violence, but you can't put out a fire of a high magnitude by blowing air from your mouth.

Testimony #12
Title/Area of Expertise: Retired Principal/Teacher
Growing up in Louisiana, blatant racism was a part of my upbringing. Whites were proud to say, "You can't come in here." As a small child, everything was separate–drinking fountains, bathrooms, even entrances to restaurants and movies. During my undergrad college days, there was a lot of protesting. I didn't do a lot of protesting because my father thought I would get hurt.

Recommendations/Resolutions/Lessons Learned
Eventually, all of the separate signs were ruled unlawful but the opinions and racist actions continued and as we see today are still in the hearts of many. There have been many learning moments for a large number of people, including me. The laws will determine the just resolutions but a change of heart and mind will determine how much learning will actually occur for us individually and collectively as a country. Being a racist is a choice. Choosing to treat people in a demeaning manner based on the color of their skin is not in alignment with what the Bible tells us. Even as a child, I could not understand why we were hated when the Bible says we should love our neighbors as we love ourselves. White people claim to be Christians too. I don't think racism will ever be resolved. Some people will always feel superior to others. This is not only with the White race but it predominates with them. As long as sin is in the world, racism will remain, but we can learn to live peacefully and respectfully with others. This is where the laws come into play and ones accepting the responsibility of failing to abide by the law. I would advise them to think about how they would feel if someone made those kinds of statements to them or a close family member, such as their mother or a sister. If they choose not to associate with someone, that's their choice, but they don't have legal authority to violate the rights of others. To avoid future happenings of this kind of behavior, practice self-control.

Testimony #13
Title/Area of Expertise: Flight Attendant (Retired), Homemaker
Many years ago, I went with a White friend to visit her parents for a long weekend. They lived in a retirement community in Paradise, CA. Her dad was the president of the homeowners association there. The association was hosting a large pool party and BBQ at the clubhouse.

My friend and I decided to go early to the pool so we could swim before it got too crowded. When we arrived at the gate, a woman approached us and very politely told me that only members were invited to the party. My friend said I was with her but the woman kept repeating that only members were allowed. She would not let me pass through the gate.

Recommendations/Resolutions/Lessons Learned
My friend's father came about 15 minutes later and told the woman that I was his guest. She backed down after that.

Testimony #14
Title/Area of Expertise: Teacher
My daughter's father loves music and we made pretty regular trips to Tower Records in Stockton, California, so he could update his collection. We all went in the store together - my daughter and I looked at the movies and then waited with her dad in the Reggae section until he found what he wanted. She was a little fussy at this point, so we decided I would take her to the car to wait while he paid. We left the store and he proceeded to the cashier with our JOINT checkbook. He placed his CDs on the counter and started writing the check. The cashier told him that they "don't take checks." He placed the CDs he had chosen in a specific spot, left the store, and came to the car to tell me what had happened. At this point, we wanted to find out if the check "policy" applied to all races. He stayed in the car with our daughter while I went inside the store with the same checkbook. I found the CDs he wanted and approached the counter to pay. I asked the cashier, "It's okay to pay with a check, right?" She said YES! At this point, I explained to her that my husband had just been in the store, attempted to purchase the same CDs with the same JOINT checkbook, and had been told that he couldn't pay with a check simply because he is Black. This racist behavior meant we would never purchase anything from this particular franchise ever again. I left the CDs and left with my family.

My husband and I never forgot this experience though and we told everyone we knew not to support Tower Records. I called and made a complaint to the manager. I am not naive and I know that racism exists, but felt so ashamed that my husband would have to deal with blatant racism in a country that SAYS it guarantees equality, but then treats people of color like second-class citizens.

Recommendations/Resolutions/Lessons Learned
As a White person, I finally understood how blatant racism affected Black men. They literally took his economic power away from him. I tend to be very idealistic about people. I've heard people say, "I don't see color," but the fact of the matter is that people make judgments and fall into negative stereotypes

all the time based on what they see. This is racist behavior. Because my ex-husband is very dark and wears his hair styled in locks, he is often stereotyped or profiled. White people feel threatened simply because of his color and law enforcement are much more likely to stop him when he is alone. LISTEN! Even if the person confronting you is angry, try to understand their frustration and anger. See past this and really hear what they are saying. Don't make light of their experience. Realize that you will probably never truly understand their experience if you are not a person of color, but you can still listen and change your own attitudes and behaviors. An inability to listen negates their experience. You are telling them that their feelings are not valid. As long as you refuse to validate their experience and acknowledge their reality, you refuse to address the realities of racism.

Testimony #15
Title/Area of Expertise: Musician/Vocalist/Music Teacher
My now-ex-husband, a White man from England, accused me of trying to turn our sons into my "little trained monkeys." He scoffed at my concerns about them being half-black with insensitive statements such as, "There you go with that color thing again!" He never helped encourage our sons to finish college. He didn't see why it was so important. He didn't even know what grants and scholarships were. Many instances such as this led me to the decision to file for divorce. Note: In the beginning, he was really sweet and put on a real good act of acceptance and admiration until he realized he couldn't control me and his jealousies and insecurities started to come out.

Recommendations/Resolutions/Lessons Learned
There is no resolution right now. My ex-husband still thinks he did nothing wrong. I tried counseling and prayer groups at church. He didn't think he needed to go to counseling. So, again, divorce. We can encourage our White friends to gently speak up if and when they observe racist behavior or comments. However, some people cannot be taught as they've been programmed from childhood. We can only be the best people we can be.

Testimony #16
Title/Area of Expertise: Senior Marketing Director, Medical Industry
I am fairly light-skinned and often not assumed to be Black. My husband (who is clearly Brown) and I were walking in San Diego's Gaslamp

District. Someone leaned into me and called me a "nigger lover." I was shocked and appalled. At first, I didn't get it. Why would they say that to me? Took me about 20 seconds to figure it out.

Recommendations/Resolutions/Lessons Learned
I was unable to respond at that point, as the person was gone.

Testimony #17
Title/Area of Expertise: Senior Marketing Director, Medical Industry
Oftentimes, people will see me and inevitably attempt to put me in a box. Given I am light, they assume Latina or something, but not them and not Black. Eventually, they will approach me and lead with a compliment (examples: Oh, you have such beautiful hair or I love your freckles) and then they ask my nationality. Since I know what they are getting at, I eventually answer with, "I am bi-racial, but identify as Black." I had one colleague take it even further and ask me why I would choose to identify as Black when I am half-white; I should identify as White. Her logic is absolutely biased... as if claiming White was better than Black.

Recommendations/Resolutions/Lessons Learned
I gently helped her understand her implicit bias.

Testimony #18
Title/Area of Expertise: Senior Marketing Director, Medical Industry
When my daughter was in middle school, a White classmate claimed to know her background without ever speaking with her, solely based on the color of her skin. He told her, her dad was probably in jail and her single mom was on welfare. She is in a home with two parents, married 28 years... one with a doctorate and the other with a master's degree. It was very hurtful for her and the entire family.

Recommendations/Resolutions/Lessons Learned
We used that opportunity to educate the child and others in the classroom.

Testimony #19
Title/Area of Expertise: Education
In 1970, at Tuskegee Institute, my friends and I were very involved in the civil rights movement in Alabama. This incident involved us being poll

watchers during an election. This one involved the governor's race. We were assigned to the city of Clio, AL, home to Gov. George Wallace, but also the home of my partner, "E". We were sitting in the polling area watching as voters came to vote. We knew George Wallace was coming, just not when. When he entered with his wife, Lurleen, he approached everyone as the press was there. He came over to E and me, stuck out his hand to shake it, and we just looked at him and never responded. This was to be his photo opp. He looked at us and in front of everyone called us "sons-of-bitches." We continued to look at him and continued to just stare at him and his antics. He was so rattled it took him a minute to redirect. We were so afraid, but showed no fear. It was a come-to-Jesus day for us. We finished our task and went back to campus to continue college life as usual knowing we had lived to fight another day.

Recommendations/Resolutions/Lessons Learned
Learning moment at the time, not to cave and be a pawn in the face of blatant racism and hate. It was well known how much the governor hated Blacks in the South. We stood our ground and lived to tell about it.
Nothing different could have been done. Speak up, no matter the consequences. If we ignore it we are complicit and a part of the problem. Educate the illiterate, if possible; if not, say what you need and move on.

Testimony #20
Title/Area of Expertise: Research Psychologist
Colored drinking fountains in 1952. In Oklahoma, I drank from the "white" fountain, which was cleaner.

Recommendations/Resolutions/Lessons Learned
We were on vacation and that time it was before the civil rights movement. I asked my parents why there were two fountains and they said that's the way it is in the South. We had traveled from California. I still remember that incident. The situation could be handled by confronting them, letting them know that is not appropriate behavior and why.

Testimony #21
Title/Area of Expertise: Research Psychologist
When I was teaching at a university, I noticed whenever I taught elective classes, that Vietnamese students would drop my class once they saw I

was African American. Later, in another class which wasn't an "elective" I was told by a Vietnamese student that, in their orientation when they came to the US, they were told Black people were dumb, stupid, and violent.

Recommendations/Resolutions/Lessons Learned
The students in the class were shocked by what officials were telling the incoming immigrants. The students began to make other Vietnamese students aware that the statement was not true. They also went to the department head to make them aware of the statement. A message needed to be sent to the department of immigration making them aware of some of the orientation that was being given to incoming immigrants that was not true, and instructing them to stop delivering that message. It's important to find out why they feel that way and where it started. Then let them know that is not appropriate behavior and why.

Testimony #22
Title/Area of Expertise: Scientists/School Board Trustee
When I first started dating my now husband, we lived in Orange County and Huntington Beach was a popular spot to go out on a date. We went there one Saturday afternoon to watch a surfing competition, enjoy the outdoors, and have dinner in town. While we were walking in town, a large 4x4 black pickup truck drove by and someone shouted something at us. We did not quite understand so we ignored it. The truck circled the block and came back, this time driving more slowly past us, they then shouted out, "Go back to the dessert you sand niggers, you're not wanted around here." I was completely shocked. My boyfriend's response confused me further. He started looking around for the other POC, because, after all, we were not Middle Eastern. To put it in geopolitical context, at that time we were at war with Iraq. I had to explain to him that that was targeted toward us. He was in disbelief until the truck circled around a third time. This time, we saw the truck approaching and we headed into a shop before it passed by. After that, we went to a restaurant. We did not want to let these racist actions bias us against a whole community.

Recommendations/Resolutions/Lessons Learned
There was no real learning at all. Afterwards, we did learn that Huntington Beach was not really a safe place for POC and we did not visit there much again.

Testimony #23
Title/Area of Expertise: Adjunct Professor/Attorney at Law
I was told that in order for me to be promoted, I needed to take the braids out of my hair. At the time, my father told me to get the position and then work to change the system from within. I changed my hair, I got the position, and then I put the braids back in my hair.

Recommendations/Resolutions/Lessons Learned
The learning moment, unfortunately, is that we have to conform to others' wishes in order to just play in the game, even if it means denying who you really are (at least momentarily). Given my age now, perhaps it would not be an issue in a lot of places. However, hair is still a determinant in many organizations and a distortion of beauty in the minds of PWIs or whom they serve (marketing) keeps them from stepping up and defending that beauty comes in all sizes, colors, and hair types. How it should have been resolved is that hair should not be the issue. Perhaps contactless hiring should become the norm.

I don't know how to solve this one until we can change peoples' belief system of what "normal" people are supposed to look like. I would invite them to attend a gathering where they are the minority, then hold a discussion afterwards, and ask their impressions of how they felt. I recommend they talk to those who are different than they are and have an open discussion of how it feels to be Black. I would ask them how they would feel if their grandchild that they'd never seen or met, turned out to be Black. I think it is healthy for them to imagine spending a day in life by opening a discussion with someone of color and discussing what makes our day different.

Testimony #24
Title/Area of Expertise: Educator
Walking across the road to my cousin's house to play, I could encounter at any moment White kids yelling "nigger" to me. I hated it. I was a little thing, so I'd get across that road as fast as I could.

Recommendations/Resolutions/Lessons Learned
I didn't have the framework to deal with this type of experience. I like to put it back on the person, ask them what is their intent behind their statement, and continue to ask them to clarify to find fallacies.

Testimony #25

Title/Area of Expertise: Pastor/Executive Director

As a child of about 10 years old, I was part of a neighborhood community center that sent inner-city Black children to spend a week with a White family in Dubuque, Iowa. The economic status of the families varied, but the family I got to visit was affluent. The father was a successful medical doctor and the mother was a stay-at-home mom. They lived in a very nice White neighborhood. They also were members of the area country club.

One summer while visiting, we went to the country club for lunch and swimming. I don't remember much about the lunch, but I remember how excited I was to get into the swimming pool for the first time. So, we dressed and went out to the pool, which was being enjoyed by many little White children. Needless to say, I was the only Black child on the property, which didn't bother me because I was with a family I had come to love. However, the moment I jumped into the pool, the parents immediately pulled their children out of the pool. The only ones left were me and two of the children from the family I was visiting. I asked Laura (a girl my age) why they got out of the pool and she said it was because I had gotten into the pool. I told her it is their problem and now we had more room to play in the water and that is what we did. We had a great time in the pool.

Recommendations/Resolutions/Lessons Learned

My learning moment was that White people do not determine how I should feel about myself. First of all, until the Lord changes every heart of those who are racist, we will always run the risk of running into racism. The way we react is all we can control. It is important that we are convinced and comfortable with who we are as God has made us. With that said, when encountering a racist, make sure you don't get pulled into the emotion of the hatred. Keep a cool head so you can approach the situation with calmness and reason.

Depending on the situation surrounding the racist interaction, if possible, try to talk with the person. If that is not possible, then talk to the authorities available when applicable, and make sure you process through the company's discriminatory policies for a resolution. In other situations you might just need to walk away to avoid possible escalation of the encounter. Remember, dealing with a wicked and unreasonable person takes a strong person to walk away and pray for their evil heart and lost soul. Seek professional or spiritual help to deal with the pain of the insult.

Testimony #26
Title/Area of Expertise: UC Merced Alumnus 2020
I have had several encounters with blatant racism within an online community. More specifically, having individuals on a video game using typical derogatory words and slander without having any knowledge of how I look, simply making such comments based on my voice. My simple reaction to this experience was removing myself from that specific in-game session or utilizing the mute function, which allowed me to block their voice communication.

Recommendations/Resolutions/Lessons Learned
There was not any resolution to this/these experiences because that person was entirely cognizant of their actions. They simply took advantage of and abused a platform that has open voice communications. Taking into consideration the established and published rules, regulations, and guidelines of this online community, such individuals should have received a permanent ban. However, the most I was able to do was file an in-game report, which ultimately doesn't have an effect on that player because it is "difficult" for these developers to justify any filed reports.

Genuinely, I feel that at this point in time, society already has a clear definition of what it means to be or act as a "racist." It all boils down to that specific individual and whether or not they choose to process their thoughts and actions before committing them; which is in turn the shocking aspect of all of this. How can we try our best efforts to make the world a better place for us all, but can't change the tendencies and decisions people make?

Testimony #27
Title/Area of Expertise: Business Owner
My experience with blatant racism started when I began traveling to the East coast and Southern states to play in tennis tournaments. Often, on the USTA Amateur Tennis Circuit, many players were hosted by local families. My stay with a White family who had children was very pleasant. However, one of the family children decided that they wanted me to meet

their neighbors. The child was only about eight years old and excited to show off his new friend in hopes of getting us some candy or a surprise treat. When we knocked at the door, an older woman came to the door and upon seeing me she immediately started yelling NIGGER and slammed the door. The child did not understand and given that I had never experienced the nigger word being called to me, I froze. We left the house and I tried as best as I could to explain to the child why the lady slammed the door in our face. I told him it was not because of him but it was because she was mean and did not like people like me. I was only sixteen years old and did my best to cover him from ignorance. I grew up in a family that shielded me and my siblings from racism as much as possible. We were encouraged to reach beyond the stars and never let anyone impede our success. Some White people may not like us but there were many people that loved us. We were encouraged to get an education and become anything we wanted to be in life.

Recommendations/Resolutions/Lessons Learned
There was a resolution of learning moments for me. I will not let anyone define me; they will have the ability to confine me. They can capture my mind and heart. So, ignorance doesn't stop the show. I think that I could have given him a Black history lesson but thought he was too young. However, I took the moment to share that I liked him for who he was because he was a nice boy and I was his friend. I could have continued to knock on the White lady's door and let her know that I was not a nigger and she should not call people derogatory names. I would recommend to a racist that I bleed just like they do. I am a human just like they are and their racist comments are more hurtful to them as well as their health. Being a racist is ignorance that has been in this country for hundreds of years. It is perpetuated through generations. We can educate racists but only God can change their hearts. "You can take a horse to the water but you can't make him drink." If only racists could see humans for humans and their ability, they can make a change within themselves. I don't know if I can change a racist but I certainly can change my way of thinking. Racism brings tension and hatefulness into an environment.

Testimony #28
Title/Area of Expertise: Business Owner
When moving to the suburbs of Los Angeles, I wanted to give my children an opportunity for a great education and diverse experience. However,

while working in the school district, I realized that the Black children were being treated differently. They were constantly labeled and were not given the same educational or leadership opportunities as Whites and Asians in the same district. I can clearly remember when Black kids raised their hands in class, they were never called on, or when it was time to line up for lunch or playtime, they were sent to the back.

I also remember the Sheriff continuously pulling my son over because he was driving while Black. Sometimes he was just getting gas or sitting in the car at a friend's house. The line of questions were not pertinent to the situation at hand. (Ex: Are you smoking? Do you have any drugs? Do you have a weapon? Do you live here?) My son was in high school at the time and had just started to drive. I immediately went to the local police station and filed a complaint. I then went to the City Councilman/Councilwoman to inform them of the harassment. I also went to our Congressmen and Senator for my area. I also went to Sheriff Baca's office to complain. After receiving the hard earned and due support, the harassment discontinued. I explained to my son that he was being targeted by the Police.

We informed him that their inadequate and belligerent behavior would not be tolerated. After watching the teachers and staff continue to treat the Black children unequally, I spoke up and let teachers and staff know that it was unfair and not the way to treat our children. Now my mission was to work in the school district and motivate as many Black kids as possible to let them know they are intelligent and can achieve. I always gave advice and hugs to brighten and lift their spirits. I eventually helped them navigate the road to college. Many are doctors, lawyers, professional athletes, teachers, entrepreneurs, and nurses, just to name a few. Many White people just don't see our worth. We are a viable piece of the American fabric. We have excelled at all levels, even as President. I refuse to promote HATE because LOVE conquers ALL!!!!!

Recommendations/Resolutions/Lessons Learned
Yes, Stop the Harassment!! The learning moment was to teach your kids that they do have options. Don't expect anything from White people. Well, I plead the fifth on how it should have been resolved. However, I could have sued the police for constant harassment. Don't give their racist action any fuel. Let them know that you don't agree with their attitude. They can avoid it by keeping their negative action to themselves.

Testimony #29

Title/Area of Expertise: Law J.D.

During a trip to Paris, my friends and I rented an upscale Airbnb with a great view of the Eiffel Tower. The Airbnb had excellent reviews on the place itself as well as high customer service reviews for the host. Through text, the host seemed very friendly and professional; she even mentioned she had a bottle of wine for us. When we arrived and she realized we were a group of Black people you could immediately notice her discomfort. She repeatedly reminded us that no parties were allowed, the neighbors regularly called the police for noise complaints, and only so many guests could stay the night. We continued to assure her we understood the rules and began to get settled in.

After about 20 minutes, she was still outside our Airbnb on the phone and eventually a guy showed up. The guy approached us and explained that our stay was cancelled, we would be refunded our money, and we had to leave. We tried to explain that we were in another country and getting other reservations wouldn't be a simple task. Without any compassion, he said, "You can figure it out at the coffee shop across the street." After that statement, we stopped talking to him and began to call corporate Airbnb. Meanwhile, the guy threatened to call the police if we didn't leave. After about 2 hours of arguing back and forth, eventually both of them said they were going to let us stay the night. Great way to start off a vacation.

Recommendations/Resolutions/Lessons Learned

The next day, I was able to speak with the manager of the two people we dealt with and I really let loose on them. I explained how their conduct was completely disgusting and that absolutely no one should be treated how we were treated, especially when we had already paid for a very expensive place. The manager was extremely embarrassed and ultimately gave us our first night and an extra night free as well as a free night at one of their other properties for our next vacation. From this experience, I learned that you don't always have to deal with another person's ignorance or bias directly; everyone has to remain accountable to someone or something. When that guy realized I wasn't going to follow his order for us to leave or fear his threat to call the police, and that I chose to speak to someone with more authority, he instantly had no more power.

I would have preferred for this situation to not have happened; however, it worked out for the better because I was able to stay calm and understand that I had more options and more power over the situation than what was being offered to me. They should have just left us alone. We weren't even in the place long enough to break any rules before they were trying to kick us out. The best way to avoid future hurtful acts that are perceived as racist is to do some deep self-reflection. Try to understand what makes you have whatever bias it is that you have, and if the person you are directing that bias towards actually did something wrong, or if it is you that has an unreasonable and unjustified bias.

Testimony #30
Title/Area of Expertise: Law J.D.
The *Roots* miniseries first aired when I was a freshman in college, and most people in my dorm watched it together and discussed it. During one of those discussions, the talk turned to affirmative action and one of our White female dorm mates opined that we (the minority students in the dorm) should be grateful because we were only admitted to UCI because of affirmative action programs.

Recommendations/Resolutions/Lessons Learned
After informing her that my grades and SAT scores were far superior to hers, my friends and I then threatened to kick her ass and she ran upstairs and hid in her room. (In hindsight, [it wasn't] the best way to handle the situation but our nerves were already raw from watching *Roots*).

Testimony #31
Title/Area of Expertise: Law J.D.
In my senior year in college, I was applying to law school and a fellow student (White female) asked me where I planned to apply. Before waiting to hear my response, she told me, "Don't bother applying to Stanford or Harvard - you won't get in."

Recommendations/Resolutions/Lessons Learned
She said this knowing nothing about me - I had a 3.9 GPA, was President of my (Black) sorority, a member of student government, and held several other leadership roles. I ended up graduating magna cum laude, being selected to Phi Beta Kappa and receiving the Chancellor's Outstanding Senior Award that year. Of course, I immediately applied to the law schools at Stanford and Harvard and ended up being admitted to both as well as every other law school I applied to. I don't know what happened to her.

Testimony #32

Title/Area of Expertise: Law J.D.

While at Stanford Law School, I worked part time doing research at the Menlo Park City Attorney's office through a school work-study program. While I was in the library (it was a small office), two attorneys started telling racist jokes in the next room.

Recommendations/Resolutions/Lessons Learned

I tried making noise (so they would know I was there) but they continued. I got up and left, reported the incident to the work-study office at Stanford, and did not go back.

Testimony #33

Title/Area of Expertise: Law J.D.

In my last semester at Stanford law school, I ran out of money and had to choose between buying books and paying rent and eating. Someone told me that the Stanford financial aid office offered emergency loans to students in my predicament. I went to the office and explained my situation to a clerk. She sighed as she got out the paperwork, saying, "You people just don't know how to handle money."

Recommendations/Resolutions/Lessons Learned

Again, I didn't handle this very well. I can only remember staring over the desk at her, yelling, and someone dragging me out of the office. (I did not get the loan, but God blessed me that day with a moving stipend from the law firm I had accepted an offer from, which covered everything I needed and still left me enough money to move.)

Military

Testimony #1

Title/Area of Expertise: Retired Aerospace Engineer

Use of the "N" word (ni**-r in the woodpile) during technical review of a complex issue in a meeting where I was the only Black.

Recommendations/Resolutions/Lessons Learned

There was an opportunity for both a learning moment and resolution. The following day, I requested a meeting with the offender to help him

114

understand. Mission accomplished! A cooling off period is preferable, except when you won't see the offender again.

Testimony #2
Title/Area of Expertise: Chief Petty Officer, United States Navy
While in the U.S. Navy (1973-1994) as a young sailor, I was new to the Navy and everyone was rotated to various jobs. I overheard my supervisor say, "Don't worry, I got several jungle bunnies and will send them to you." I was amazed that it was said so casually. I told my senior about it and was told, "Don't over react, that's just the way he is." Nothing else was done, I continued to work, and stayed in the Navy. Things did improve over the next two decades.

Recommendations/Resolutions/Lessons Learned
My learning moment was when I had joined the, which was predominantly White. I quickly realized that I would have to deal with some racism and sexism and needed to choose my battles. I believe that my supervisor should have been called out, or put on report for using racial slurs and unprofessional conduct. Let the individual(s) know that you are insulted/offended by the language or behavior. Ask them to stop and report them if they don't. Take notes of the incident, tell the truth, and be timely.

Testimony #3
Title/Area of Expertise: Electronic Technician
Being short in stature, besides being BLACK, I have had to turn the other cheek and be better than others to be considered average. But that did not hinder me from excelling in almost everything I endeavored to do. I was the last one chosen for a team, the last one hired, and the first one fired. The majority of my working career, I was the ONLY Black man in the group, disliked by both Black people and White people. I worked among White people and had to take my breaks with the Black people. Even as a Black man with a BA degree, I could NOT advance [the same] as others without a degree. I witnessed too many Black men and their families ruined by RACISM of the United States Armed Forces! They would only let Black men be cooks or deckhands through the 1960s.

Recommendations/Resolutions/Lessons Learned
I advanced rapidly in the U.S. Navy being an Electronic Technician Radar 2nd Class and the first Black man to transfer from Radar Operator School to

Electronic Technician School. Though I am not a famous person, I hold many records for being the first Black man to achieve different goals.

Non-Black

Testimony #1
Title/Area of Expertise: Paralegal and Law Student
I am a lighter skinned Puerto Rican and Mexican. So, unlike my father who is significantly darker than me, the chances of being specifically targeted in a racist act have been reduced throughout my life so far. I also grew up in a different time than my parents. It wasn't uncommon when my mother had rocks thrown at her by other children who called her "beaner" in the 1970s. Even as a Latina, my lighter skin and relative youth have afforded me a certain privilege, but that doesn't mean I haven't seen, been offended, or been demoralized by racist acts.

What impacts me the most are the stereotypes and racist lies I hear about Latinos. We aren't smart. We are lazy "illegals" who aren't even U.S. citizens and should go back to our country. According to our current president, we are even rapists and drug dealers. These false depictions of people in my community and family anger me. People who automatically think this way don't understand who we are or where we come from. I know countless Mexicans and Puerto Ricans who are strong, hardworking, and family-oriented people. We care about our own and will do everything we can to protect and provide for them. Racism makes it easier to ignore these truths and scapegoat groups of people for problems that are not their fault. We must fight to change this.

Recommendations/Resolutions/Lessons Learned
Racism hurts people. It destroys families and communities. If you want to avoid being a racist and eliminating your implicit biases, it's going to require work. Be open to discussing and hearing new thoughts and feeling uncomfortable. Before changing policies, we have to change culture and the way we talk about race issues. Learn more about the origins of marginalized groups and how current inequities in the fields of education, healthcare, criminal justice, and employment stem from colonialism and slavery.

Educating yourself about the problem is the best way to begin understanding. Once you've learned enough about the problem, you can take action in your community to support politicians who are vocally anti-racist and committed to changing the way certain policies and laws negatively affect marginalized groups in your city, state, and country. Hopefully, by doing this together, we can make the world a better, more equal, and just place.

Testimony #2
Title/Area of Expertise: Retired
In 1973, I was 15 years old, and I had given birth to a baby girl. My Catholic parents refused to let me bring her home, essentially kicking me out. I ended up at Booth Home in Oakland. It was a home for indigent women and their children run by the Salvation Army. It was also my first real exposure to systemic racism and White privilege. It was the first time I heard the terms "Cracker" and "Peckerwood." The "N" word was used as part of everyday vernacular. There were around 40 women at Booth Home. The ethnic make-up was primarily women of color, Black and Brown, with very few White women. We were all poor, homeless, and out of alternatives. The women there received no money for basic necessities. Many were prostitutes or serious drug users trying to find a way to make a better life and keep their kids.

Some of the women I talked with couldn't read well or do basic math. The system was designed to keep them right where they were, turning tricks or dealing drugs just to buy toothpaste or feminine hygiene products. Months went by and I made friends with the women there. Systemic racism was evident in overt and insidious ways. The staff was always encouraging me, but my friends didn't get these pep talks. I believe I was treated differently because I was White. I was young and cute. I had the benefit of a good early education; I had just fallen on hard times. Booth was not where I was supposed to be. That sadly was not the assumption for many of my Black friends.

Recommendations/Resolutions/Lessons Learned
My experience at Booth Home had a profound effect on me. The effects of lifelong poverty can eat away at a person's spirit and will. Without believing you have an achievable path to a better life, what's the point?

Police

Testimony #1

Title/Area of Expertise: Clinical Psychologist

Probably the most blatant [act of racism] occurred when I was 26 years old. I had just finished working at a preschool in La Canada, CA, and always ate lunch in my car for 30 minutes because I had a class to attend and this allowed me time to relax before driving to my class. We could park in the lot that was also shared with the elementary school. On this particular day, I did the same thing I always did–got ready to leave. Before I could pull out of the parking lot, I was stopped by the police.

I couldn't figure out what I could have done since I hadn't left the parking lot and I knew I had turned on my signal light. His first question when he came to my door was, "What were you doing?" I looked at him and answered, "What?" He repeated his question and stated, "I saw you sitting in there. What were you doing?" I explained that I was having lunch and that I worked at the preschool. I can't remember if he asked for my license and registration or not. I know he paused and then let me go.

I remember feeling worried about how long he had actually been watching me. I usually sat in my car for 30 minutes, no problem. I will say this is something that other people have done as well and it is the agreed upon place that parents use for parking their cars, so it's not unusual to see people there.

Recommendations/Resolutions/Lessons Learned

It did cause me to be much more aware when police are around. Not that I had not been, but that one was really blatant. I've had other nonsensical stops, so I'm now more prepared when they happen. It shouldn't have happened or if he really was concerned that there was a problem, he could have talked to me while I was parked.

Police can be clearer with their concern. Example, "Why are you in this parking lot having lunch and not somewhere else?" Again, I could tell him that I work at the preschool and could have verified it, if he were concerned about the children, although there were no children around. Actually, there was no one around at the time.

Testimony # 2
Title/Area of Expertise: Medical Support Assistant
As a high school student, I was walking home and was stopped by police. Due to the fact that high school had just got out, a lot of high school students were walking home as well. The police stopped all of us and demanded that we tell them what we were doing walking around the area. I was wearing a solid blue shirt and the police assumed that I was in a gang. I sat on the curb for 45 minutes being grilled by Sacramento PD officers. I sat there, remained compliant, and repeated all my previous statements to their questions.

Recommendations/Resolutions/Lessons Learned
There was a resolution–somewhat. The officer eventually let us go and I went home and told my mother. From that day on, I knew not to wear solid blue or red in the neighborhood because police would always assume that I was in a gang. I also changed my walking direction to school to separate myself from a large group of kids. The situation could have been avoided altogether.

The cop shouldn't have stopped everyone considering we were around the corner from the local high school. The amount of kids who live in that neighborhood is astronomical, but instead, they thought we were a gang walking around the neighborhood looking to wreak havoc. Police should try to remain open and understanding. Don't be so quick to assume or play into stereotypes.

Testimony #3
Title/Area of Expertise: Leadership
I was asked by the police how I could afford such an expensive car during a traffic stop. I cautiously answered the policewoman's question. Racial profiling – stopped by the police six times for false traffic violations. Reported to the court and made to pay the fines.

Recommendations/Resolutions/Lessons Learned
No solutions and no positive learning moments. The judges believed the police officers' statements that I committed the violations. I'd ask officials to treat others how they would want to be treated. Also, how he/she would want their family members to be treated by others.

Testimony #4

Title/Area of Expertise: Education programs

I was driving through a predominantly White, upscale neighborhood en route to work. Approximately a mile or so from my destination, I noticed a police car sitting at a stop sign as I passed. Moments later, he was following me and shortly thereafter pulled me over. The first thing he asked was, "Where are you going?" which meant to me that I should not have been in that neighborhood. He went back to his vehicle and I assume he did a check on me. Upon returning, with my license and registration card, I asked why he stopped me. He said my "brake light was out." He didn't give me a ticket, just said, "Have a nice day." I didn't know if he was telling the truth about the outage, but being stopped numerous times for similar reasons, I believed his motivation was my race. The way I dealt with the situation came from the teachings of my parents when I first got my license. Keep your hands on the steering wheel and comply. Upon arriving at my destination, a co-worker and I checked for outages. As I suspected, all lights were working.

Recommendations/Resolutions/Lessons Learned

There was no learning moment to speak of. I relied on the decades-old advice of my parents when dealing with the police; keep hands on the steering wheel and comply. This is a very difficult question because it incorporates numerous possibilities/scenarios depending on the context.

Testimony #5

Title/Area of Expertise: Telecommunications

One night, my fiancé and I were returning to my parents' house. We were at a stop light when a police car pulled up alongside us. I glanced over at the officer and turned back around. I told my fiancé that he was going to pull us over. He disagreed and said we had not done anything wrong. I told him again that he was going to pull us over and not long after he flashed the lights on us. My car had a temporary registration and I thought that was the reason he was going to use as to why he pulled us over. So, he came to the window and as I rolled the window down I started explaining the registration and handed him the paperwork. He then asked my fiancé to step out of the car and told me to stay in the car. The officer took him to the back of the car and started asking him questions. As I looked in the rear view mirror, I could see another officer on the passenger side of the police car with his gun drawn. I was very nervous and scared for my fiancé. The officer came back to my window and asked if he could look in the trunk. I got out of the car and went to open the trunk. Meanwhile, they have taken my fiancé over to the passenger side of the police car where the other officer had his gun drawn.

As the first police officer searched the trunk, the other officer patted down my fiancé very hard as to try and provoke him; I could see his body move with every pat. The officer searching the trunk did not find anything and told me I could get back in the car. I told the officer, "I will wait until you are finished with him." The officer looked at me then went over to the other officer and they talked and came back with my fiancé and told us that the reason we were stopped was because there was a robbery at 7-Eleven and he fit the description of the suspect. Then they let us go. Also, during all that time they never questioned the temporary registration.

Recommendations/Resolutions/Lessons Learned
I felt that my telling the officer, "I will wait until you are finished with him" took some of their power away and possibly stopped the situation from turning bad. I think they could have just checked our identifications to confirm who we were, if there truly was a robbery.

Testimony #6
Title/Area of Expertise: Retired
I was going to St. Mary's College getting my Master's; I was 49 years old. After class ended one night, I got in my car and headed down the road to the freeway. I noticed a police car following me; no lights were on to signal me to stop or anything. After driving about –five or ten minutes, I made a left turn heading to enter the freeway. It was after I went down the ramp to get on the freeway, the policeman turned on his lights signaling me to pull over. I pulled over and he approached my car asking for my license and registration.

I complied saying nothing and he went back to his car. Momentarily, he came back, returning my license and registration. At that point, I asked what this was about and he said a car like mine had been stolen. He went back to his car and I drove off.

Recommendations/Resolutions/Lessons Learned
I shouldn't have been stopped in the first place.

Testimony #7

Title/Area of Expertise: Health and Fitness Trainer and Nutritionist

One afternoon, I was standing in front of my home. Two White male police officers pulled up without any cause and started questioning me saying that I fit the description of a guy they were looking for. As we went back and forth about the wrongful incident, for which I didn't fit the description, they went on to ask my name. Since this situation wasn't a peaceful one, I denied giving my name. They called their commanding officer, who also pulled up and said that I must have a police record as long as his arm because no Black man they know has not been in jail. They assumed I probably had a warrant, but because I was standing inside the gate on my property, they couldn't detain or arrest me. The back and forth went on for almost an hour before they got a call and left.

Recommendations/Resolutions/Lessons Learned

As I stood my ground, I explained to them that it's so disrespectful to assume anything about me just because they didn't have my name and I stood for what I believed. Eventually the situation calmed down, but I won't say we agreed on anything. I still never gave my information and we came to a respect level that afforded an apology. As a result of the misunderstanding, they gave me their badge numbers and names and that was the end of it. The learning moment was that because of the color of your skin you can already be guilty of something you've never done. I believe they could have come up to me respectfully, asked my name, explained to me what the situation was and it wouldn't have gone that far. When you're dealing with someone who doesn't look like you, don't intentionally treat them any differently than how you would want to be treated.

Testimony #8

Title/Area of Expertise: Sales, Marketing, Promotions, Event Planning

I worked for the *Wall Street Journal* delivering papers in the middle of the night to customers in Redondo Beach by 5:00 am. I had to be at the distribution center at 12:00 am. I had to get my papers, fold, rubber band them, place them in a box, and double stack them in the front and back seat. Once completed, I proceeded to my route. Because of the time of morning and how I was trained, you drive on both sides of the street and make sure the paper is in the driveway. While I was driving, doing my route, I noticed the Redondo Beach Police following me. I kept doing my route because the papers had to be delivered by 5:00 am. I arrived at a cul-de-sac and four Redondo Beach Police cars pulled up with lights shining on me. The officer walked over to the car and asked me what I was doing. Keep in mind, I'm being followed by the police. I proceeded to answer him by stating that I worked for the *Wall Street Journal* and I had to complete my route by 5:00 am. My car was double stacked with papers in the front and back seat. At the time, the *USA Today* had just come out and it was a very colorful paper. I would always grab about three or four. I just happened to have them sitting in the front seat next to me and gave the officer one. He let me go and we all went our separate ways.

I was going to Palomar Junior College San Marcos, CA, in 1975. My father lived in Inglewood so my roommates and I decided to rent a car and drive to Inglewood to spend the weekend with my family. There were four of us in the car. Someone more familiar with Southern California made a suggestion that we go to Third Street Promenade in Santa Monica. We were just about there when the Santa Monica Police started following us. We pulled over. I was sitting on the passenger side and the officer came up to the window and asked the question of where did you steal this car? I told him this car isn't stolen, but rented. I explained to him, I'm a college student attending Palomar Junior College in San Marcos, CA. This car was rented in San Diego and I'm here for the weekend to spend time with my family. I pulled all the rental documents from the glove compartment to prove what I stated. We were asked to exit the car and sit on the curb for one hour while they ran our ID and couldn't find anything. We just sat there until they realized they had nothing and let us go.

Recommendations/Resolutions/Lessons Learned
Because I grew up in Detroit I had my experiences, so for me you keep your cool, listen and answer the question with calmness knowing you haven't done anything wrong. I should have never been stopped because nothing had been done to warrant it. No matter where I lived, and in some cases, if I'm not aware of my environment, any wrong thing or question can escalate into a situation that may have a bad outcome. This is a very important time in our history where people need to be educated on the realities we face. In spite of being educated and successful, we still have to deal with a system that is designed to systematically benefit another race and minimize elevating us to positions of authority, due to a fear of influence, power, and the ability to inspire change.

Testimony #9
Title/Area of Expertise: GM Information Management
While at work back in Washington, New Jersey, I was stopped during my lunchtime by police who asked me if I lived or worked in this area. I asked why. He remarked that I seemed "lost or a long way from home!" I was shocked, but again not surprised! I told him that I manage a company here and the owner's name is Ed. He responded by saying that he knew him, but was not aware that I was working there. I showed him my business card and driver's license and thereafter I was allowed to leave for work.

Recommendations/Resolutions/Lessons Learned
The resolution was that I provided him with my business card and driver's license. I made it simple by providing him with the appropriate documents. As Proverbs 15, verse 1 states: "A soft answer turneth away wrath, but grievous words stir up anger."

Testimony #10
Title/Area of Expertise: Electrical Engineer
I once took my daughter to a music practice and was waiting for her in my car, parked in a parking lot. While waiting there, I was hit by a White lady from behind. She did not admit hitting me and tried to leave the accident. When I tried to stop her from leaving, she called the police. The police arrived and put me in the back of their car, despite me being hit from behind. They blindly believed her. They talked to her in her car, not in the back of the police car. After they completed talking to her, they checked my driver's license, registration, and insurance.

Once they completed checking, they started questioning me. After politely explaining what happened and showing them the paint of the car that hit me, they started to believe what happened. It was frightening to be treated like a guilty person without assessing the situation without bias. They left after they made us exchange our insurance. This incident shook me ever since. This happened because I was Black, in my [opinion].

Recommendations/Resolutions/Lessons Learned
The incident was resolved by explaining the accident in a polite manner and making them understand logically what happened and pointing out the evidence to them. I don't know if there is a learning moment from here. I just understood that Black people are guilty until proven innocent. The

police should have treated both of us equally rather than assuming I was at fault without discussing what happened. Racism is deeply rooted in American culture and propagated through the media, Hollywood, and ingrained in the culture. It takes a lot of work through education, change of curriculum, and willingness of the other side to be open-minded, and listen and learn. People miss the big picture of why issues exist in our society. The systemic racism that exists is the main cause of a lot of the problems that exist in society and it takes a long time to reverse the damage.

Testimony #11
Title/Area of Expertise: Analyst/Organization Development
My husband and I were driving through our neighborhood, which was predominantly White and affluent and a police car followed us for a while before flashing his lights for us to stop. They pulled up next to us and asked if everything was ok. We said yes and he went on to ask where we were headed. My husband responded "home." He looked at our car and said, "Nice car, is it yours?" I was beginning to get angry, so I asked in a very defensive voice if we did something wrong to warrant getting signaled to stop. My husband touched my arm to get me to calm down and answered his question. I was fuming with tears in my eyes and blurted out, "Is that all?"

Recommendations/Resolutions/Lessons Learned
No, there was no resolution. The police officers should have never profiled us. I can't think of any recommendations at the moment because I am all in my feelings and fed up with racism.

Testimony #12
Title/Area of Expertise: Manufacturing Manager
I was stopped on many occasions in various cities (Newbury Park, Thousand Oaks, Moorpark, Simi Valley, Encino, and Culver City) and asked why I was in the area. I remained calm and non-aggressive while answering all questions in a non-intimidating manner.

Recommendations/Resolutions/Lessons Learned
The learning moment was this was a no-win situation and being angry or aggressive would not be beneficial for me. My thoughts are, "Don't stop

me because I'm a Black man in a predominantly White neighborhood and because you believe I do not belong there." It may be helpful in similar situations to let them know how their words are being perceived.

Testimony #13
Title/Area of Expertise: Educator
As an English Language teacher in a San Diego high school, I experienced the following. After a Friday night football game, a fight broke out between Caucasian football players and Latino males. The following Monday, two deputies showed up at school and were escorted by an Assistant Principal to the classrooms to locate the students who were in the fight. From across the hall, I watched as the football players were brought out into the hallway, where they stood around talking to the deputies about their last game. The deputies then approached my classroom and called for five male students. They took those students out into the hallway, ordered them to kneel and put their hands behind their backs, and handcuffed them. The freestanding football players and the handcuffed Latino students were walked through the school, across the quad, into the discipline office.

Recommendations/Resolutions/Lessons Learned
After several days, no individual student was found at fault. I never heard anything more about the incident from the deputies or school administrators.

Retail

Testimony #1
Title/Area of Expertise: Human Resources Manager (Retired)
When I was about 16 years old (about 1962), in Rockwall, TX, my friends and I stopped at a roadside hamburger place. We wanted to order food, but were told they "didn't serve niggers." One of my friends responded that, "We didn't want to order niggers, just hamburgers." At that age, the only thing we could do was leave.

Recommendations/Resolutions/Lessons Learned
The only thing that incident solidified was that, as African Americans, we had to be aware of what places we were allowed to visit. We were living

in a segregated society and had grown up being told that some places were off limits to us because of our color. In that time, where segregation was the norm, we did not feel we had any power. We should have been able to report the incident to someone, but it was understood that businesses could choose to serve us or not. Now, I would tell them that words matter. Rather than make a general statement about any group, ask yourself how you would feel to hear the same comment about yourself.

The first time I visited California, I thought there would be no discrimination. However, I found that in the West or the East, discrimination is just not as overt as the South. I found racism in places that wouldn't hire me and in places that didn't want me to sit down. It was disheartening to learn that folks pretended to be color-blind, but in reality just found other ways to keep me separate.

Testimony #2
Title/Area of Expertise: Lawyer/Administrative Law Judge
I went to a restaurant in Marina Del Rey. When we approached the host, one said [the restaurant] was closed. We asked if it closed early. He said yes. We thought it strange that a major restaurant would close early. We waited to see if others would be allowed in to dine. As we suspected, they were allowed in for dinner. We called it out immediately and wrote several letters.

Recommendations/Resolutions/Lessons Learned
We got an apology, but nothing more. The host should have been questioned, trained, and/or fired. People should educate themselves and be open to courageous conversations to increase their sensitivity

Testimony #3
Title/Area of Expertise: Health Care
When I was 15, my family and I were traveling to Tennessee State University for Homecoming and stopped to eat at a Waffle House in Kentucky. I was the first to walk in and immediately the hostess/waitress walked off and said to another, "You help them, I'm not." I was quickly saddened and knew immediately that she didn't want to serve me because I was Black.

Recommendations/Resolutions/Lessons Learned
The other waitress helped my family and I chose to not eat. She should have been fired. It is important to remember that we all bleed red and are made up of the same components. We are all human beings.

Testimony #4
Title/Area of Expertise: Senior Data Analyst
A few years ago, I went to a restaurant with a coworker (who is White), in a city that is mainly White, within Ventura County, California. When we walked in and got a table, there was a group of older White adults having dinner. They all stopped eating and started staring at me. Then one of them said to me, "What are you doing here?" I politely replied that I was here to enjoy a nice dinner just like them. The man then scoffed and went back to eating his food. My friend asked me if I knew them. She didn't recognize the blatant racism that just happened.

Recommendations/Resolutions/Lessons Learned
Some people will be racists and unless they choose to reach out and understand other cultures, they'll never change. I could have engaged with them, but thought it's not worth it. They were strangers. If I engaged with them on a regular basis then a conversation would have been warranted. You can engage with them and listen to what they have to say, and then try to change their opinion.

Testimony #5
Title/Area of Expertise: Property Manager
I went to a grocery store in New Jersey in a predominantly Spanish community. A fair-skinned Latino came up to me and started speaking in Spanish. Even though I understood what he said, I replied in English. He then proceeds to ask me if "the watermelons are good this time of year." I did not have a watermelon with me in line waiting to check out. This was clearly a bigoted comment, so of course my response was not nice. However, I did not reply with a racial slur. The entire interaction occurred in front of the store clerk who was also a fair-skinned Latino male. Even though the first guy came up to me and started a confrontation with me, I was asked to leave the store without the items I came to purchase. I believe that if I had a lighter complexion that comment would not have been made and I absolutely would not have been asked to leave the store.

Recommendations/Resolutions/Lessons Learned
I learned about blatant racism pertaining to a culture I was not used to. Before that incident, I didn't realize Afro Latinos experienced racism. I believe I should have reported that store and followed through with a resolution. I am positive that I was not the first or the last person with melanin to get kicked out of that store. I didn't not see any signs that read, "We reserve the right to refuse service to anyone" and since they had no good reason to kick me out, I should have reported the incident. I would advise them to put themselves in our shoes. If they wouldn't enjoy the nasty comments or injustice being hurled at them and their people, they shouldn't spew it out at anyone else. The golden rule of life, do unto others as you would want them to do unto you.

Testimony #6
Title/Area of Expertise: Educator
I went to a Best Buy to buy some movies when I was about 20 years old. My friend in front of me wrote a check for his movies (he is White). I attempted to write a check and was told that they "don't accept checks from 'your kind.'" I had to pay in cash.

Recommendations/Resolutions/Lessons Learned
I should have spoken up, but I didn't. Understand that all people are different. When you make assumptions, they are usually wrong. Get to know people, not ideas.

Testimony #7
Title/Area of Expertise: Entrepreneur - Manufacturer
I politely told the sales clerk the price is not a problem and that I would like to purchase the item.

Recommendations/Resolutions/Lessons Learned
For me, the learning moment was they assume [because] you're Black you can't afford it. I should have told her, "Why would you mention the price right off and assume I could not afford it?" I believe people need to be educated and not judge us because of the unknown. My racist experience was during my four years at a Catholic school that my three sisters and I integrated.

Testimony #8

Title/Area of Expertise: Administrator

There are a few, but what sticks out most is when I was a child at the Dadeland Mall. My brother, sister, and I wanted ice cream from the stand in the mall. My sister was nine and I was six years old. Our mother gave us money to go get the ice cream while my aunt and mother chatted for a while. When we went to the stand, we were told they were closed. We left and went back to where my mother was and she inquired what happened. We told her they were closed, as we looked in the direction of the stand and observed them serving some White children. She said they are not closed and had us return only to be told again they were closed and then served another group of Whites once we left. My mother then went over and I can only imagine what she said. Needless to say, we left without ever being served.

Recommendations/Resolutions/Lessons Learned

Learning moments at that age should be positive and not confusing. Why hate or mistreat someone without cause? Learning should always be a positive outcome experience. Negative outcomes are damaging and usually nothing good comes from them. I believe the people behind the counter should have been struck by a lightning bolt. Not sure why, but I believe hate without cause usually comes from internal ignorance. My experience with people like that is they are usually too ignorant to understand anything you would say to them.

Testimony #9

Title/Area of Expertise: Retired Supervisor (USPS), Production Worker

This happened while visiting a newly opened grocery store (ALDI) in Montgomery, Alabama, in 2019. I had recently had shoulder surgery, so my right arm was in a sling. I gathered my groceries and went to check out. I noticed there were prices next to the bags. I asked the cashier if I had to buy the bags and she said yes. I picked out two bags (enough for my groceries) and set them in the top of the cart where she could reach them. She started ringing my groceries up and proceeded to set them on top of the bags. So, I ask, "Am I supposed to bag them myself?" Her answer was yes and she continued ringing them up. Mind you, I have my dominant arm in a sling. So, I pull the bags from under the groceries and start to bag them. She finished ringing them up, asked me for payment, and told me I could finish bagging in the area they had for bagging. At this point, I see a White manger watching and he doesn't say a word. I'm thinking and saying out loud how rude they are, not considering that I'm handicapped. The same White manager sees an older White customer at the next register and asks if they need help. I was so upset I vowed never to shop there again (which I haven't) and decided since they were advertising the new store on social media I would post my experience.

Recommendations/Resolutions/Lessons Learned
After posting under their ad, someone responded, but he wasn't trying to resolve anything. He made a statement that I shouldn't judge the store because it was newly opened. However, someone should have shown some compassion while I was in the store and at least asked if I needed help. After the fact, an apology is always good. Just acknowledge your wrong doings and treat people as you want to be treated.

Testimony #10
Title/Area of Expertise: College and Career Readiness Specialist/Education
While in college studying for my undergrad degree, I would regularly visit the mall next door to eat, study, or shop. This particular day, I visited the Forever 21 and to my dismay and shock, I was being followed. Immediately, I felt hurt and uncomfortable. Years passed and I found myself back in retail at a luxury outlet. While profiling was prohibited, we were constantly given store policies that clearly said the opposite. I would constantly watch and hear in my ear (we had walkie's) as African Americans were profiled, told to leave large purses and shopping bags outside of the fitting room as store policy (this was done to African Americans at high rates), and folks were called to "customer service guests" which was code to make sure nothing was being stolen. One of the associate's friends had been called out while I rang him up. This was extremely traumatic for me and one of the final straws. Here I was, a Black person being made to profile another Black person, despite understanding how traumatic this experience could be. All I could feel were tears.

Recommendations/Resolutions/Lessons Learned
For retail, there needs to be a better dialogue around how to not stereotype non-white customers. Acknowledge your privilege and change. I find that most White people that I work with in education are problematic. Yet, because they may have a Black significant other or child, teach African

American students, are liberal and voted for Obama, and even march in a protest, they're okay. No, you're not. Racism, I feel at times, is looked at through a broad lens by White people as if they cannot perpetuate racist behaviors and attitudes in very intimate spaces, especially work. But this happens all the time. I would also say, speak up if and when you do see this.

Testimony #11
Title/Area of Expertise: Education
An older Caucasian woman pulled up behind me at a gas station. There was space for her to pull up into two open stalls in front of me. However, instead, she began honking and yelling for me to move so she could pull up. She then started driving closer and threatened to hit my car. It didn't matter what I wore, whether I was a professional, it didn't matter that she simply could have pulled up to the other spaces in front, she just wanted what she wanted as a convenience for her and expected me to just comply. Privilege.

Recommendations/Resolutions/Lessons Learned
Learning moment with the gas station. It escalated. The more vocal I became the more calm they became. They threatened to call the police, which I was okay with. However, in this day and time it may have resulted in a biased outcome. Fortunately, I had a witness who stepped in and talked to the person and told them to back off politely. She should've gone to another space, plain and simple. Take unconscious bias training. If it's really not the intention read up on racism. If it's really not the intention, educate yourself.

Testimony #12
Title/ Area of Expertise: Educational Diagnostician
When I was in grad school, after I completed a paper that took me an extremely long time to complete, I decided to go to a nail salon to "treat" myself to a pedicure. It was 5:00 PM and the hours of operation on the door indicated that they closed at 7:00 PM. I went inside and there was one customer, who was being serviced by the one nail tech in the salon. As soon as the nail tech saw me, he stated that they were closing early. I said the sign said that they closed at 7:00 PM and he said, "Yes I know what the sign says, but I'm leaving after her service is done." I then said,

"How about you put a sign up that says 'Whites Only.'" The White woman sitting in the chair turns to me and yells, "Get your Black ass out of here!" I was furious. I told her to go to hell. I immediately left and called an attorney friend of mine.

Recommendations/Resolutions/Lessons Learned
There was no resolution. I wound up going back to the salon a few days later to retrieve the nail tech's license number. He did not remember my face (which indicates that he does that a lot). After getting the number, I sent a letter to the Texas Cosmetology Board with my grievance. I never received a response.

Sports

Testimony #1
Title/Area of Expertise: High School Football Coach
I was about 10 or 11 years old; can't remember exactly. At that time, I was living with my grandparents. I had an aunt that was two years older than me (let's just say my grandparents loved each other). At that age, I was playing Pop Warner football and basketball, as most young men did during the 1970s. My aunt was a cheerleader and she wanted to be a dancer. She danced in competitions and would come in first or second place all the time. She found out, in the neighboring city (a predominantly White city), there was a dance studio that produced and prompted several careers for their students through Disney. One night, I overheard my aunt asking my grandparents about attending this studio. My grandmother was on my aunt's side in her attending, while my grandfather was okay with her attending the current studio she was in. My grandmother ended up convincing my grandfather in letting my aunt attend. So, my grandparents made it happen.

Within a couple of days, I came home from basketball practice, and my grandmother sat me down. She tried to convince me that my aunt needed my help at the dance studio because no one in her class studio could do the lift at the end of my aunt's routine and she felt that I was strong enough to do the lift for her. Of course, I said no. My grandmother continued to try to convince me that my aunt really needed me. I kept saying, so does my team. My grandfather comes in and he says, "You are not playing basketball this season. You are going to that studio and you're gonna learn this routine." When my grandfather spoke in his home, everybody knew it was law. So, I went the next day and learned the routine. I still know that song to this day... "Hello my baby, Hello my..." A boy from Compton shouldn't know that song. We competed in the showcase and came in third place, which, now I question, LOL.

Mrs. Perkins, a White lady that worked with my grandmother, and her granddaughter also attended the studio. She was having a pool party for everybody after the showcase. So, we get in the car and go over there. My grandparents have a pool in their backyard, which went from 5 to 13 feet deep at a slope and 30 yards in length. This was before all the regulations came about for pools. My cousins and I swam every summer in this pool and developed a tradition. We tried to [swim] from the shallow end to the other end while holding our breath for as long as possible. As I enter the backyard of Ms. Perkins, I'm looking at their pool and it's about three-quarters the size of my grandmother's. I'm excited, because I know I can go from one end of the pool to the other while holding my breath and make it. So, there I go in the shallow end and take off. I'm underwater and I make it to the other end, do a flip-turn, push off, and start towards the shallow end. So, now I'm coming out the other end. I'm back on the shallow end and I touch the wall. I come up and throw my hands in the air! I look around and everybody is out of the pool except for Ms. Perkin's granddaughter. I wipe the water off my face with my hand, and I hear Mrs. Perkins telling my grandmother, "I'm so sorry, I didn't know."

My grandmother comes into the shallow end of the pool, grabs me by the arm, and pulls me up the stairs of the pool, right out the backyard gate with my aunt right behind us. Mrs. Perkin's was still saying, "I'm sorry, I'm so sorry... I didn't know." My grandmother turns to Mrs. Perkins and says, "These are my grandbabies, my grandbabies, you should have known." My aunt and I get in the car and my grandmother drives off. I'm sitting in the backseat, still trying to dry off, still confused. I asked, "Grandmother, why did we have to leave?" I said, "I don't understand grandmother, what did I do wrong? Did they think that I was gonna drown? You and (my aunt) know that I can swim." My grandmother said, "That's not it baby." She said, "I knew you could make it and I knew you were going to do it before we walked in the backyard." She said, "They didn't want to be in the pool with you sweetie." And I said, "What?!??" She said, "Yeah, baby. They didn't want their kids in the pool with you." I said, "Why?" She said, "Because you are Black."

I finished drying off in the back of the car. About a minute later, I kinda laughed to myself as I asked the question out loud, "Donna didn't need me because I was strong. Donna needed me because I was Black." My grandmother said, "And strong." Now at family gatherings, my aunt and I just tell the story about the time we came in third place at Showcase Studios in Downey, California.

Recommendations/Resolutions/Lessons Learned
No, for this particular situation there weren't any identifiable resolutions. The learning moment, at the time, is that this is what I have to deal with. This is what I am up against. It has never been resolved. I don't think, at the moment, it could have been dealt with. I don't think, in the days to come, it could have been dealt with. I think, since then, my aunt and I deal with it by describing the fun we had dancing at Showcase Studios during that time. Listen to the person who you may have offended without interrupting them or trying to explain that is not what you meant. Let them finish. Then, find a way to ask, "Can you help me find a better way to say what I am trying to say, so I don't sound offensive?" This way it can be a teachable moment.

Testimony #2
Title/Area of Expertise: Government Executive
I moved to rural Arizona as a teenager and it was my first set of experiences with overt racism. Several people called me nigger during the two and a half years I was there. One incident stays with me. I had caught the winning touchdown pass at the end of a football game. One of my teammates, exhilarated by the victory, ran up to me and told me what a great nigger I was. I don't remember what I did or how I handled it, actually, but it stayed with me.

Recommendations/Resolutions/Lessons Learned
I don't have recommendations other than to do some introspection and reflection.

Testimony #3
Title/Area of Expertise: Police Officer
I can't recall a blatant racist experience I'd had before I became a police officer. Since I've been a police officer there has been plenty of times that

I've been called a "nigger" by some civilian I'm dealing with. I deal with it by smiling and laughing because I'm usually arresting the person and their words don't affect me at all.

Recommendations/Resolutions/Lessons Learned
Racism is taught. No one is born a racist. It is like a family generational curse that needs to be broken. The only way to avoid it is to break the cycle. My advice would be to start asking the people who taught them to be racist some questions. Like, what made them hate someone because of the color of their skin? Have they ever tried to get to know, understand, or befriend someone with a different skin color? Why do they think someone is less of a human being because they have a different skin color? Why are you afraid of a skin color? How can you be a Christian but hate someone because of their skin color? Since there are racist "Christians," I think a racist should start there and then go on their own to befriend and get to know someone of a different race. They'll find that some people with different skin colors are just like them. They may grow fond of another culture and be able to experience different ways of life. They may learn something from another race to better their lives. Overall, they'll see that there is absolutely no reason to hate someone and think of them as an animal because of their skin color.

Testimony #4
Title/Area of Expertise: Doctoral Candidate
Some onlookers at a soccer game I was participating in said things like, "She can't run fast with her braids so tight." I did not respond.

Recommendations/Resolutions/Lessons Learned
It would have been difficult to halt the game, but perhaps some sort of negative statement or action would have sufficed.

Testimony #5
Title/Area of Expertise: Educator
[I remember] playing high school basketball, having the crowd chant the "n" word when I touched the ball.

Recommendations/Resolutions/Lessons Learned
I finished the game, and was upset about it later.

Workplace

Testimony #1

Title/Area of Expertise: University Director/Administrator, S.D. Co.
Social Services Administrator and Program Manager (Retired)
I have had several blatantly racist experiences and lost opportunities during my lifetime. I have been profiled several times driving and shopping while Black, and reported the incidents to police departments and store managers. In Detroit, my children could not play on the playground closest to our home because it was on the border of the White community in Dearborn, MI. My husband, who is White, chose not to accept a lucrative position in Mobile, AL, in the 1980s because he feared how racism would hurt me and his three Black stepchildren. I wanted to be a photojournalist in high school. My counselor nicely told me to "get real" and become a teacher or social worker!

I will elaborate on this experience: While working as a program specialist for the Co. of S.D., my supervisor very angrily stated to me, "You are late getting back from your event (which was a conference for Black women). I should give you twenty lashes!" This same woman had made other remarks like, "Next time we'll ask Vonnie to bring the chicken for pot luck! She probably knows the best places!" The twenty lashes incident was the last straw for me. I remained calm, gathered my belongings, interrupted a meeting of executive staff, and announced that I would be leaving work immediately and not sure when or if I would return because I had been subjected to yet another racist comment and was too emotionally distraught to work. I threatened that I would also be filing a complaint with the civil service commission and writing an email to the Director and Board of Supervisors.

Recommendations/Resolutions/Lessons Learned
The email to the Director produced a long tearful apology from the supervisor to me by phone at home and pleas not to report the incident to the commission. She stated that I was among her best program specialists and that she was having a very bad day. I was given three days off with pay and an apology and praise from the execs for how I handled the incident. She received a severe reprimand, warning with possible termination for more incidents, and mandatory cultural awareness training. We had a few discussions about race and about her family being

anti-black but she certainly did not perceive herself as a racist. I was sick and tired of educating White colleagues on blackness and chose only those I thought worthy of my efforts for serious discussions. She was not among them. I was soon promoted over her in another department. She sent me a nice congratulatory note. I was tempted to contribute a coupon for a bucket of chicken for her retirement party, but my grandma taught me better than that! I was satisfied with the resolution mainly because her new attitude and behavior toward me was to my advantage. I received the best assignments and was never again confronted or questioned about ANYTHING. A report to the commission is very serious and may have caused her to retire early or be fired. Our White female manager who is married to a Black Jamaican acted quickly as did our White male manager who needed me to ghost write his reports and was not about to see me quit or transfer! All good!

It depends on the individual. Some folks are beyond redemption! Generally, I would advise that you keep track or even document the offenses and have a private conversation with them about how you felt hurt and how offended you were. Also, use it as a teachable moment about what is acceptable and what is not. Our S.D. County cultural training sessions were very good and beneficial for those of us ready to receive the info and educate ourselves.

Testimony #2
Title/Area of Expertise: Senior Payroll System Analyst
I was at work and I had a question. A White male manager was passing by, so I caught his attention. When he came to my cubicle he said, "Yes monkey, did you want something?" I was so taken back I did not know how to respond nor what to do.

Recommendations/Resolutions/Lessons Learned
I mentioned this only to my friends at work. There was no resolution and to this very day, I regret that I did not speak up! I did not go to my direct report or HR. My learning lesson... SPEAK UP! I should have reported the incident. I should have spoken up! In retrospect, I would have let them know that the remark or action is racist and ask them not to say/do that again!

Testimony #3
Title/Area of Expertise: Asset Manager/Commercial Real Estate
I was living in Newport Beach, CA, and was in the midst of returning to work. I applied for a position, had a wonderful phone interview, and was offered the job. When I arrived, the person that I had spoken with on the phone, a woman wearing a necklace with a Star of David charm, met me in the receptionist's area of her office and informed me that there had been a mistake and the position was no longer available. I thanked the woman, and extended my hand to shake her hand, which she did not accept and I walked out of the building. Yes, I experienced a range of emotions, and remembered my beautiful brown skin is not welcomed in all circles. I am sure I was hired sight unseen primarily due to my alma mater. Most importantly, my paternal grandfather is Jewish, and my last name had definitely created a conundrum.

Recommendations/Resolutions/Lessons Learned
It was clear to me in 1990, as it is in 2020, that racism is alive and well. The way I handled the situation- maybe I should have taken out an article in the Orange County Register. Although, reporting a private employer's racism in 1990 may not have had a lot of steam. I'd advise to place the situation back in their lap.

Testimony #4
Title/Area of Expertise: Paralegal/Inclusion Special Education
I was working for a non-profit and we had a fleet of company vehicles. The cars were to be cleaned and fueled up upon return. I returned a car that had been previously driven by a colleague who was non-Black and was not cleaned. I was told by the supervisor that I was responsible for cleaning the car. I informed her and the attendant that I was not the responsible party and that I was returning it for that very reason. I was told to clean the car or be written up, which I had never been. It just so happened that after my supervisor walked away, the VP was walking by and saw that I was upset and inquired about my demeanor. I informed her about what happened and she informed me I did not have to clean up after my colleagues.

Recommendations/Resolutions/Lessons Learned
Working for the non-profit, I was told that I was not responsible and did not have to clean the car. I should have received an apology from my

supervisor. They should take some implicit bias training, enroll in a Black studies course, and ask questions to a friend or someone who they trust about their thoughts before acting.

Testimony #5
Title/Area of Expertise: Retired
I worked on a job for almost thirty years. Nine years in, I felt I was more than qualified to try out for a position one pay grade higher. So, I put in my request that I was interested in trying out the position. There were five of us who ended up trying out for the position. When it was all said and done, I was one of two chosen to be interviewed a second time. I felt my interview was exceptional, thinking I had the job. One reason was the other candidate was someone I had trained when they were hired. The company ended up promoting the other candidate over me. The other person was a White woman who had come to the company after me. The pattern of the company was that they hired people of color, but they were not quick to promote them even if they were qualified. After my experience, I talked to my supervisor and the Union. I told them how I felt about the whole thing. I let them know I felt I had been discriminated against. It didn't get anywhere. They encouraged me to keep trying. They did promote me the next time. For the almost thirty years I was there, people of color who were more than qualified never were promoted right away. This was their way of keeping their knee on our neck and making us feel like we were less than.

Recommendations/Resolutions/Lessons Learned
Don't let your situation stop your ELEVATION, because the Lord always has your back. The first sentence is a family quote. Eventually the people of color who worked there got tired and started making noise to ensure they were heard. We have to speak up and let them know they're wrong. We can't sit back and let it go. Many times, they don't even know they're making racist statements, mainly because they've done it for so long. We cannot allow them to do this any longer. Sitting silent is over.

Testimony #6
Title/Area of Expertise: Teacher
I was at my job longer than another worker. When a position came open, she received it without it being put out for everyone to go for it.

It should have been open to all workers. In the future, I'd be sure to speak up when I see things are not fair.

Testimony #7
Title/Area of Expertise: Licensed Medi-Cal AOD Case Manager/DOC (Criminal Justice System)
I was visiting the store that I used to work at. One of my old managers saw me and asked if I could assist him with customer questions. My former manager, who is Caucasian, was very pleased to see me and politely asked if I had a minute. I said yes, I would answer questions if I could. Before the manager could get the question out of his mouth, the customer said loudly, "We do not want a 'nigga' helping," then looked at me!

My old manager was so embarrassed he apologized! I said, "Let the ignorant asses figure out their own question," while I looked in their eyes! The manager and I walked off after he told the customers we don't need your business.

Recommendations/Resolutions/Lessons Learned
Actually, yes, there was resolution. My former boss called me to say that the couple came back to the store to apologize at a later date and still needed help. The manager told the couple that he stopped me while I was shopping to ask if I could answer questions because he was not sure. The manager told the couple that the former employee always would have a job here because she traveled to many store locations and trained all staff including managers, and how much wealth of knowledge she has regarding this line of work.

They told the manager they wanted to apologize to me personally if he could get me back in the store. I said no at first, but then I said I wanted to see their faces when they apologized! I set a date and time at my convenience. They were there waiting when I arrived. They shook my hand, gave me beautiful flowers, and apologized profusely. Me being the bigger person, I told them what they needed to know and they ended up hiring me for consulting on a project they had because they found out I was also a licensed designer and a professional. Lesson learned, sometimes you give people a chance to come down off their racial issues!

Testimony #8
Title/Area of Expertise: Payroll Professional
During this time, Obama was running for President. On Election Day before leaving work, my manager (who is White) stated, "I know who you are voting for." My reply was, "I am voting for the President whoever will be elected."

Recommendations/Resolutions/Lessons Learned
My learning moment was that she was racist, and it came out with what she had to say. No resolution was achieved. Being the manager of the department, I think she should have apologized, but of course, that didn't happen. I think you should think about what you say, and try and put yourself in their shoes.

Testimony #9
Title/Area of Expertise: Principal
I was the only Black employee in the Planning Commission Department in San Carlos in the early 1980s. As I went into the community to inspect building permits, I was denied many times. Community members would demand to talk to my supervisor. In the mid 1980s, I worked as a district sales manager for Chrysler Corp. Once again, I was one of the few African Americans who worked for the company. I was often placed in districts where there was a lot of prominent racism. I felt like I was put in these locations purposely to be set up to fail. I was never placed in a district that I requested, and often was told that I was not wanted in those locations.

Recommendations/Resolutions/Lessons Learned
I was laid off in San Carlos. I filed a lawsuit against Chrysler for racism and they settled with me out of court. In both incidents, conversations should have taken place with me directly. Training should have been done at the companies. I recommend approaching the person from a place of wanting to educate them, letting them know that systemic racism still exists, share experiences with them, and let them know that their actions are hurtful and why they are hurtful.

Testimony #10
Title/Area of Expertise: Veterinarian
I was a teenager working in the Lucky Market produce department. My White assistant manager called me a nigger. I happened to be holding a

knife in my hand. I laid the knife down because I knew enough not to want to go to jail that day. As I was walking toward him, God had the store manager walk into the room and ask if there was a problem. That immediately diffused the situation. I let it be known that if he did it again I would hurt him.

Recommendations/Resolutions/Lessons Learned
There's never resolution and they are all learning moments. I should have kicked his butt. For people that are truly unaware of their racism, be open to hearing what Black people are trying to tell you. Don't get your feelings hurt or get defensive. Listen and work to change accordingly.

Testimony #11
Title/Area of Expertise: Veterinarian
I was working at Disneyland in the horse stables. I was taking care of the horses that pull the streetcars on Main Street. I wanted the job because I loved Disney and horses. I wanted to be one of the streetcar drivers. I would ask my supervisors repeatedly when I would be trained on the streetcars because that was the natural progression of my job. I was always given some excuse - the most honest answer they gave me was that they wanted to stay "true to the period." Then December came around and my manager was excited to tell me that the Christmas parade theme that year was Song of the South. The organizers found out that the stables had their first Black keeper and they wanted to know if I would like to be Uncle Remus and lip sync Zippity Doo Dah in the Christmas parade while driving a team of two mules. I quit. Never had much use for Disneyland since.

Recommendations/Resolutions/Lessons Learned
Decide how committed you are to being a better person. If you're down when it's black and white (George Floyd), but you step into the shadows when it's a little grey (Rayshard Brooks)... I just need to know which person I'm dealing with. I won't hold it against you if you're not fully committed because I never expected any commitment in the first place. I just need to know.

Testimony #12
Title/Area of Expertise: Director/Student Affairs
I applied for a lead position in a 3-person unit where I would be the third person and the other two people in the unit were also Black. I had been

working in a Minority Engineering Program, but prior to that, I had been an admissions recruiter where I first did minority recruitment, but then moved on to honors. During the interview, the interviewer said that given my background with minority students, how would I be able to relate to little Sally (White) from Idaho? I guess she missed the part of my background that showed where I went to school (PWI), my role in recruiting honors students (some minority, but 95% were not), and my overall professionalism. I later learned that she commented to the "team" that there was concern with having three Black women in the office. The woman they would eventually hire was White and someone I had trained in a previous office.

Based on her questions with my ability to work with little Sally from Idaho, I knew I wouldn't get the position. I was actually ok with not getting the job because I had always had great/comfortable work environments and if this woman was this small-minded, I didn't want it. The other women in the office were disappointed because they had worked with me and thought I would be great.

Recommendations/Resolutions/Lessons Learned
I was still young enough in my career to not deal with it even though it was clear what she was doing. The older, wiser me would have known to push back and challenge this, potentially even going to HR about the question and overt discriminatory assumptions that she was making. I should've called her out on it and then reported her to HR. At the heart of being racist/making comments is a lack of understanding and a judgment that is based on their biases. Advice would be to listen with your ears and not prejudge an individual.

Assumptions were made because I am a Black female that grew up in a Black community and preferred to work with minority students. While this was indeed a preference, it did not define who I am nor what I am capable of doing... she assumed it was. When you make assumptions like that, you miss out on incredible candidates. There are many instances that we let slide off our backs like water on a duck, but that doesn't mean that it doesn't hurt and makes us feel demeaned. I am nearing the end of my career now and have nothing to lose, so it's easier for me to say something. A conversation that lets them know specifically what they said/did and the impact of the words/behavior can be used as a teachable moment.

Testimony #13

Title/Area of Expertise: IT Project Manager

When I was eighteen, working a summer job for Social Security, as I was working alongside a White coworker, I scratched my head because of an itch. My coworker said, "What are you doing?" Susan then proceeds to say, "Oh, yeah you're thinking." I immediately reported her actions to our manager who reprimanded her.

Recommendations/Resolutions/Lessons Learned

I learned to stand up for myself and not allow others to look for any type of flaw or derogatory action with me. I believe this situation was dealt with immediately by my manager because the company wanted the races to get along. I would tell them to darken their skin and put a hooded sweatshirt on then walk into an exclusive department store to see how the sales clerk would treat them. Then ask them how they would feel to be treated like this every day.

Testimony #14

Title/Area of Expertise: Social Justice/Ethnic Studies

Several years ago, while working for a former employer, I was forced to participate in a celebration of Black marriages, while none of my other colleagues were asked nor expected to participate. I was the only Black person on staff at the time. Ironically, a few months later, there was a celebration of Latino marriages and only my Latino coworkers were asked to participate. I even asked to participate as this event appeared to be more fun than the Black marriage event and I was told that I was needed for another event. Fortunately, a member of the executive team noticed my anxiety, anger, and frustration and brought it to management's attention.

Recommendations/Resolutions/Lessons Learned

The first issue resulted in an employer sponsored diversity event, which actually opened the door for us to have some difficult conversations, but really did not change the racist culture. This incident at least attempted to change the environment, but it did not go far enough. Racism should be declared a mental health crisis. I have learned that I have been traumatized by racist experiences and that these experiences determine the places I go, where I choose to live and work, and the forms of entertainment I enjoy. Post Traumatic Slave Syndrome is real.

Testimony #15
Title/Area of Expertise: Social Justice/Ethnic Studies

While working with the same employer, I was assigned to work in a part of town where I have had a few racial incidents and I asked to be reassigned to another work location, as I did not feel comfortable working at this location. This area of the Sacramento region is known for racism. I did not feel that my request was out of line because this employer had a reputation of accommodating employees. My racial discrimination concerns were compared to gender discrimination and "unfortunately these things happen." I was shocked and totally dismayed when I was written up and given a different work assignment, which was practically a demotion. This issue was resolved by karma as the agency lost its funding about two months later.

Recommendations/Resolutions/Lessons Learned

This issue was never resolved and forever changed my professional relationships. I did not feel understood or heard. I wish somehow the individual oppressing me would be able to spend just one week as a Black person. Correct the comment and let people know that words can hurt. If people would just take the time to learn about another culture, ethnicity, or nationality, they would realize how much we all have in common. We all have our own historical journey and perspective. No one story diminishes another story.

Testimony #16
Title/Area of Expertise: Lead Avionics Technician

After an Honorable discharge from the U.S. Navy, I returned home to Los Angeles, CA, and was employed by IBM in 1966, the year of the "Watts REVOLUTION." I was the only Black man in my group. IBM exploited my position and sent me where others were afraid to go. When I quit IBM and moved to the Bay Area, I was blackballed for a number of years from obtaining Technical employment. I managed to ask the Mayor of San Francisco on ABC TV to help me get interviewed for jobs at my skill level. I was refused employment by United Airlines and hired by Pan World Airways and became the first Black man to work their Electronic Shop. My most rewarding experience was with Trans America Airlines. I was the Avionic Technician with a crew that flew an L130 Cargo aircraft in Angola, Africa. I was the first Black man the Angolan people saw work on an aircraft, and they LOVED me! Everywhere I went, people stood in awe of me. They wanted to help or be around me! Schoolchildren would run along the school fence to talk or touch me. Man, I felt 10 feet tall!

Recommendations/Resolutions/Lessons Learned
My supervisor at World Airways would send me to Travis Air Force Base every night! For a long time, I thought it was because he didn't like me. Then people told me that he sent me because "I was the BEST." I NEVER had an airplane delayed or cancelled flight. He depended on me to keep his job.

Testimony #17
Title/Area of Expertise: Lead Avionics Technician
When I was in junior high school, I moved from Los Angeles to Compton, CA. This was my first real remembrance of RACISM! The first thing I did to fit in was to "jump on a White boy" walking home from school. There was a White gang called the "Spook Hunters." On the back of their jackets was a Black boy kneeling down, begging for mercy, with a White boy standing over him, with a chain in his hand! We would fight them up and down Compton Blvd. every Friday night after the football games at Compton High School. I went to Centennial High School. After a basketball game with Paramount High School, at Compton High School, I took a branch from a tree and hit a player from Paramount across his head. The following Monday at school, two twin brothers and I were expelled from every high school in California for "exciting a riot."

Recommendations/Resolutions/Lessons Learned
I managed with the help of GOD to enroll back in a school in Los Angeles. I don't think the twin brothers ever finished school. Sometimes YOU JUST HAVE TO FIGHT to stop hurtful actions from happening in the future! By any means necessary! Otherwise, they will bully you all your life. Many times, I have gone to the supervisor to no avail. They are White also and sometimes they stick together! I have lived almost 80 yrs, NOTHING HAS CHANGED!!!

Testimony #18
Title/Area of Expertise: Truck driver
Even though I had more seniority and skills for a position, I had to work twice as hard to be acknowledged.

I've learned that the system is working against African Americans. Treat everyone fair and educate yourself.

Testimony #19
Title/Area of Expertise: Medical Social Worker/Masters in Social Work
Last year, my employer (of 5 years) hired a new Social Worker Supervisor. She's a White woman from San Mateo. At the time, I was the only person of color social worker (on the home health side). The others were White like the supervisor.

At our home health social work meetings, the new supervisor would make announcements of changes that affected our daily work schedule. She was developing new programs that meant our workload was going to increase significantly.

My White colleagues and I spoke up and expressed our concerns. We didn't need more work. We were already overwhelmed. Her response to my White colleagues when they expressed questions/concerns was always so kind and sweet. She addressed their concerns and listened to them. When I asked questions or shared my thoughts, her tone changed. She was rude and spoke down to me. It was clear that she did not respect me or see me as an equal. This continued for months. My workload continued to increase until I physically got sick because of how stressed out I was. I had double the cases of everyone else. My supervisor knew this and allowed it to happen for months.

I started communicating my thoughts, concerns, and questions via email. Instead of talking to the supervisor on the phone or in-person, I wanted to keep a paper trail. I started documenting the numbers of cases vs. my White colleagues weekly to show that the workload was not evenly divided. I wanted to track her rude responses and disrespect. I wanted to show that she was treating me differently than the others. I strongly believe she is racist. How am I different from my colleagues? I'm a person of color, mixed/bi-racial, Black and Mexican. I'm not White.

Recommendations/Resolutions/Lessons Learned
I learned that we must always stand up and speak up against racial inequalities. At the workplace, it's hard, but very important. In my case, I

went to HR and filed a complaint against my supervisor. I printed out all of my emails to show that my complaints were valid. Later, I learned that three social workers of color from the hospice department also filed a complaint against her. We collectively requested a meeting for us to meet with HR and together we reported everything. I think people should try to understand and accept their own privilege first. That's hard, but necessary to avoid hurtful actions from happening again.

Testimony #20
Title/Area of Expertise: Executive Administrative Assistant
My first time with racism was working for a stationery company. I was the only young Black woman working for the company. Billy, my manager who was White, was leaving the company and was nice enough to inform me that the new manager, John, didn't like Blacks. It really didn't faze me too much because Billy had promoted me to the book department, and I was so excited about the makeover I was going to do to this department. As a few weeks went by, John stopped by to observe the store. This was his first time at the store and he didn't know any of us except for Billy. When John entered the back of the store, he decided to observe the book department; as he was looking over the bookshelves, he found an old book. John asked Billy who was managing the book department. Billy told him, and John asked Billy to call me to meet with them. I proceeded to the back of the store to meet them, and when John saw me, he started turning different shades of red; again, he didn't know I was Black. I can't remember Billy having a chance to introduce us, from John yelling at me regarding an old book. I didn't know what to do. I felt as if daggers, lynching, and verbal name-calling was all in his yelling. I remembered walking to the break room crying so hard, I could barely breathe. I've only cried like that once in my life, and that was when my cousin Marvella died. It was horrific the way he spoke to me. One of the ladies I worked with came to the break room, and asked me if I wanted her to kick his ass; she was Samoan. I told her no, it was going to be okay, and if anything, he would probably fire me.

After five to six months of working, and John not speaking to me, he calls me to the office. I told my friend Robin, "It's been nice working with you," thinking he was going to fire me. Instead, he asked me to be his bookkeeper. I took the job. John trained me; sometimes working late nights by myself. It was just the two of us in a small office. There was no talking; he was a chain smoker, and just a miserable man. After four months working with him, he asked me if there was anything I wanted him to do or change in the office. Before I could say anything about his smoking, he said, "I'm not going to quit smoking." I said, okay. The next morning, he brings in several machines to take in the smoke from the cigarettes.

After another month, he started talking to me, and it was my opportunity to ask him if it was true he didn't like Blacks, and he said, yes. I asked him if he saw me... I said, "I'm Black." He said, "But you're different." I told John NO, I am not different; there are good and bad people in every race. John proceeded to tell me about his childhood and how his father called Black people every dirty name under the sun. People are not born racist, but many are taught to become racist such as John. I've carried John throughout my life, and have shared this story in college, on the job, and to police officers. It is always amazing to see people's faces when I tell them the 360-degree change John made.

Recommendations/Resolutions/Lessons Learned
The resolution with John was he was willing to change to become a better person. John came to my wedding. Derrick, my husband's side of the family is very fair, and my family is dark. John came to South Central, walked into the church, went to the front, and sat with the dark people. He gave me a Love Spectrum book with his signature 'Love John.' After I left the country for a few years, I returned home, and needed a job. I called John to see if he had any openings, and at this time, he was now a District Manager at a different store. He asked me if I wanted to be his bookkeeper, and to come to the store to fill out an application. When I arrived at the store, he had hired all Black women. I couldn't believe it. John, and I truly went through a process, and we learned from each other. I knew God was carrying me, and I'm so glad I didn't give up on him. It was resolved through prayer, staying quiet, listening, and learning on my end. John is my story for life. I know God can change hardcore people like him through prayer. My recommendation for a person who is racist is to try to build a relationship outside their race. Take time to learn about Black or other cultures. If that doesn't work, get help and talk to a professional, or even better, read the Bible. If people read their Bible they would find, we are all first cousins, and why would you want to hurt family?

Testimony #21
Title/Area of Expertise: Claims Adjuster/Litigation
I was a young management trainee with F. W. Woolworth located in El Cajon, CA, in 1988. I was the only Black employee on the payroll. As a trainee, I worked alongside other White assistant managers and my assigned mentor was the store manager. From day one, their body language conveyed disappointment when they saw me. As a trainee, I had questions, but other assistant managers were not eager to provide answers and the store manager failed to provide clear instructions on how to complete certain tasks. I had to learn by error during several circumstances. At the time of my progress reports, I was told that I took too much time completing tasks that my peers could do in half the time. The manger implied that I might have a reading/learning disability. He said sometimes these issues are overlooked when "affirmative action" is exercised. The store manager did not think I had a future in store management, but he recommended that I work and oversee the "snack bar/hot food" because "fried chicken" was their best seller. I told him I was not interested in handling only the "food" section of the store. I earned a degree in business management, and I was qualified to continue training to be a store manager. He then proceeded to tell me that I would be better at "selling cosmetics out of a suitcase."

Recommendations/Resolutions/Lessons Learned
I learned that no matter how hard you try, for some people, you will never be good enough because of the color of your skin. I believe the manager should have provided the tools and training needed for me to successfully complete the training program. The manager should have been more of a mentor, utilized interpersonal communication skills, and worked to have an inclusive work environment.

Testimony #22
Title/Area of Expertise: Director Facilities/Operations
I worked in an office with another African American woman. We both were supervised by a Caucasian woman who often referred to us as "you people." When confronted about it she simply said it was her little pet name for us.

Recommendations/Resolutions/Lessons Learned
Educate yourself. Research the history.

Testimony #23
Title/Area of Expertise: Retired Educator
In a business meeting, my boss made comments regarding the superiority of White women to Black women.

Recommendations/Resolutions/Lessons Learned
After I replied to the comment, he dismissed the others from the meeting and tried to apologize for the comment.

Testimony #24
Title/Area of Expertise: Manager, Community Engagement and Strategic Partnerships (K-12 and Higher Education)
For more than eighteen years, I worked for one of the nation's most influential K-12 education organizations. I joined the company at age thirty and rose through the ranks of Executive Director of more than twelve states and was responsible for a $32 million budget. My team met our goals every year and I helped the company expand critical programs at the district and statewide. Yet, when it was time to move up to the next level, I was met with constant resistance and blatant racism. Despite my stellar career, outcomes, and performance, when it was time for an opening for Vice President in the organization I was met with a NO. I prepared for my internal interview with the Senior VP. As an internal candidate, he didn't give me the position and later hired an incompetent man that I had to train. I went to HR and complained that as an internal applicant, I wasn't given any feedback as to why I wasn't hired for the position. After meeting with HR, the Senior VP said, "We need a unique set of skills at this unique time."

Recommendations/Resolutions/Lessons Learned
I learned to stay true to myself and my commitments.

Testimony #25
Title/Area of Expertise: Marketing
At age 21, going on 22, I arrived in San Francisco in the summer of 1972 armed with a college education, and the optimism and naivety only youth can conjure up. Fast-forward four months. The Employment Development Office had sent me out looking for mostly administrative or secretarial positions, Monday through Friday, without success. Each time I was sent

to an employer, usually along with three other young women, all White, I would be the only one coming back without a job offer. This happened over and over again. I was told that I was overqualified, so I left my college education off, and then I was told I was under qualified. By this time, the money I had was just about exhausted. I was renting a room at the YMCA and every dime I had went for rent and sometimes for food.

It was fall now and getting close to the Christmas shopping season. I thought I would be able to find something during this time. A young White lady staying at the Y told me that one of the premiere department stores downtown had started hiring for Christmas and she had gotten a job for the season. When I arrived at the store, I went directly to the personnel desk. I started telling the young woman there that I was looking for work, but before I could finish my sentence, she interrupted and said, "I'm sorry, we're not hiring." I asked her if she was sure, to which she rolled her eyes, and responded, "Yes." Still not willing to accept my fate, I asked if she knew when the store would be hiring. She sighed as if she was at the end of her patience with my inquiry, and mumbled that she did not know. When I got on the elevator to begin my journey back home, there was another African American woman a few years older than me. I was still pondering my fate, really talking to myself when I said out loud that I couldn't believe they were not hiring. She immediately asked if they told me that they were not hiring. When I confirmed that's what I had been told, she said, "Here, take my card, I'm an assistant buyer here. You call them tomorrow and tell them that I referred you." She went on to complain how they (the White people) had their children, nieces, and nephews working there over the holidays, but they didn't want to give jobs to Black folks who needed them. I thanked her, and did exactly as she told me.

This time they gave me an appointment with personnel and I was hired! This particular store had one room upstairs where all sales transactions were reconciled; that's where I was assigned.
First day on the job, I arrived 30 minutes early. I wanted to make a good impression. My supervisor was off work that day and my co-workers, two White women and one Chinese woman, decided they would be my supervisors for the day. They had me doing every transaction, and seemed to enjoy not doing anything but bossing me around. The day went by fast and at day's end, they actually complimented me on how quickly I caught on.

The next day when I walked into work, I extended a morning greeting to my co-workers, but noticed they barely spoke and they had strange looks on their faces. I cleared my throat, and out of the inner office area, I heard a voice say, "Go to the infirmary." I leaned in to see the person ordering me to the infirmary. I saw a middle aged, dark haired White woman, and I said, "Good morning." I assumed she was the supervisor. She did not return the greeting but said, "I told you to go to the infirmary."

I followed her instructions and immediately left the office headed for the infirmary. I explained to the nurse in the infirmary that I had only cleared my throat. She took my temperature, which was normal, gave me a small supply of cough drops, handed me a slip, and sent me back to work. As soon as I opened the door to enter my office, the middle-aged lady told me that they wanted to see me in personnel.

When I arrived at personnel, the same woman was there. I told her that my supervisor said that they wanted to see me in personnel. She said in a matter of fact manner, "We're going to have to let you go." I managed to ask, "What do you mean, why?" She said, "Your supervisor said that you have a bad attitude." As I began to explain that my supervisor had only seen me for less than five minutes, she couldn't possibly have come to that conclusion, without warning and before I realized it, tears were falling down my face. As I wiped them away, she simply said, "I'm sorry."

I was very aware that in those few moments that I had been discriminated against and rendered an injustice that was indeed the most hurtful experience of my life to that point. The supervisor's bias towards me and her willingness to be so cruel as to lie, and cause someone that she didn't even know to lose her livelihood was incomprehensible to me in that moment. I wanted to tell someone and ask for their help. I thought of the NAACP and went to a phone booth right in the store and called them. Unfortunately, my case was a small matter. They told me it would be a few months before they could even see me.

It occurred to me that I should at least thank Cheryl, the woman who gave me her card and got me the job. I wanted to say goodbye and for her to hear what happened from me and not someone else's version. I called her and she asked me to meet her upstairs in the cafeteria. I told her what happened. She asked me point blank if I had taken any money. Offended, I told her of course not. She asked me to wait for her there and she would be back. She came back in about 30 minutes and told me that the Vice President of Personnel wanted to see me in his office. I met with the Vice President and the first words out of his mouth were, "You have a job." I was so relieved, the tears started to flow. Handing me a tissue, he told me that he understood that I had a very unpleasant day and he wanted me to take the next two days off with pay. I was reassigned, and this time I worked in the basement at the employee entrance where they left their personal items and purchases from the store.

Recommendations/Resolutions/Lessons Learned
Although it was actually resolved, the person who committed the act did not even know what happened in this instance. She should have, at a minimum, been brought in for a conversation. I was just one person she did that to. Without even being called out about it, she has probably done it to many more people of color. The only learning moment would have been that the person who resolved it was the same race as the person who committed the offense. So, it reminds us that not all persons of a certain race are insensitive to racial issues.

Testimony #26
Title/Area of Expertise: Former Engineer
I interned at Brady Corporation in Milwaukee for three years before I was hired as a full time employee. At that time, Brady prided itself with having a woman as their CEO and advertised about their value in diversity. As an intern, the chemists and engineers taught me the procedures and processes of innovation through new product development. They were gracious and supportive. The moment I became a full time employee, the demeanor of many employees in Research & Development flipped. They didn't speak to me until they needed information or a question answered. Some technicians told my manager that they didn't want to work under me. There were even two situations where I presented an idea to a team and it was ignored. Months later, another team member presented that same idea and the team decided to go forward with trials. In those meetings, I stated that I presented the ideas months ago. The manager would find ways to twist what I said and deliver it as if the idea was not feasible. I even found out that a colleague who held the same position as me was making more money. He bragged about how much he was making to a group of colleagues. I was upset because he was making almost $6,000 more than me. This same colleague was hired a year after me and interned less years

than me. I spoke to my manager about it. He ignored me. I then went to someone in HR. She secretly told me that the other colleague was getting a raise about every four to six months. The range of the raises was from $0.60 - $2.00. Raises were supposed to be given once per year.

Recommendations/Resolutions/Lessons Learned
I eventually arranged to have a meeting with the VP of Human Resources and stated that I would contact the EEOC for an investigation if this was not rectified. I was given a $7,000 raise, but the treatment I received never changed. I ended up leaving the company after three years of service.

Testimony #27
Title/Area of Expertise: Driver
I am from Senegal, West Africa, and I have been in the U.S. for a little more than twenty-two years. In 2006, I became a contract driver delivering products for Office Depot. I had worked for them in the past as an employee; and enjoyed such a good work reputation that when they laid off their employed drivers, they offered me and a few others an opportunity to have our own businesses and still deliver their products. I financed a box truck and began my work with them.

I'd been working for about six months when I delivered a file cabinet to a medical company in Alameda, CA. As it turned out, the file cabinet was not the correct one for the size files they had. The procurement clerk was a Caucasian lady and she complained about receiving the wrong file cabinet. I apologized to her even though the drivers do not select or load stock onto the trucks. I took the cabinet back and told the department responsible that it was the wrong cabinet. The lady had also called Office Depot to complain as well.

A couple of days later, a file cabinet was again loaded onto my truck for delivery to the same place. Unfortunately, again it was the wrong file cabinet. This time she was livid and called Office Depot to again complain. I took that file cabinet back. The next day another file cabinet was loaded and I delivered it. This time it was the right one. She asked me to wait to see where the person she ordered it for wanted it placed. She came back in about fifteen minutes and told me to just leave it where it was because the other person was on a conference call at that time.

When I came into work the next morning, the dock manager told me that the lady from the Alameda medical company had called and complained that I didn't put the file cabinet where she asked me to. I told the manager that she must have forgotten what happened and I would talk to her and remind her of what happened since I had a delivery for her that day.

When I arrived at the medical company, I delivered the article I had for them and while the procurement clerk was signing for it, I asked her if she remembered telling me to leave the file cabinet on the dock because the lady who ordered it was busy at that moment. She said that she remembered and was very pleasant about it. I politely informed her that my boss was under the impression that she was not happy with where I left it. I then left and went about my route.

About an hour later, I got a call from my dispatcher telling me to come back to the warehouse immediately. When I arrived at the warehouse, I was told to turn in my badge and Office Depot wanted my truck off their property as soon as possible. He told me that the lady at the medical company called and said I confronted her and she felt threatened. I suffered a lot of hardship, financial and psychological, behind that lady's lie. I lost a $136,000 contract, I was unemployed for a while, I was paying for the truck, and I never again had a salary to match what I made then.

Recommendations/Resolutions/Lessons Learned
As soon as I got home, I told my wife, who is African American, what happened. The first thing she said to me was, "Honey, why didn't you talk to me before you went to talk to that White lady?" She went on to tell me that she would have told me not to even say anything to that woman. She told me that Black men have been killed because of White women lying on them; and when calling the authorities, they know that their word will be taken over any Black man's word. That was my learning moment.

Testimony #28
Title/Area of Expertise: Principal Engineer/Capital Projects for Pharmaceutical Companies
This isn't something that happened directly to me, but to my team. On our project team, we sit in a construction trailer. It's an open space and when there are a lot of people there, it can get loud. I have two men from Puerto Rico currently on my team and when they're working together, they speak

Spanish. A colleague from my department (not a contractor) took it upon himself to yell at these contractors one afternoon for "speaking too loudly" around him. Everyone in the trailer is loud, including this guy. One of the contractors texted me while I was in a meeting to let me know what was happening. Many other people witnessed this event as well. I spoke to my colleague, where he continued to complain that the contractors were too loud and he couldn't concentrate. I didn't get to speak to the Project Manager until the next day, when he told me he'd heard about the incident and spoke to this colleague. The colleague and the Project Manager are both White men with outspoken conservative views. The Project Manager told me that my colleague admitted the issue was that the contractors were speaking Spanish and he didn't understand what they were saying. They were talking to each other, not him, and we don't have any policy requiring anyone to speak any particular language in conversation at the company. Documentation has to be in English, that's our only requirement.

Recommendations/Resolutions/Lessons Learned
For me, this only confirmed previous microaggressions and hostility coming from this colleague. There was no disciplinary action against him. In fact, I had to investigate how I could move my team away from him. Since then, he refuses to work with one of the contractors.

Testimony #29
Title/Area of Expertise: Navy Weatherman
I was working on an asbestos abatement construction job site (military barracks) in Arlington, VA, not long before I joined the Navy.

The crew, close to a dozen or so laborers, shared rooms (two to each room) in a motel out in town. I was sharing a room with a White guy at the time. He had come from the hometown of the owners of the company in North Carolina. One night, the guy went out in town, and got drunk. He came back that evening agitated (raising hell). I was trying to sleep (we both had to work the next day). We got into an argument. One thing led to another, he called me a nigger, and I punched him in the face. We got into a wrestling match and a couple of the guys from the work crew came over to break it up from next door. I slept in another room that night. Afterwards, I was at peace.

I wanted the money from the job and I definitely wanted the job. But, at this point in my life, I was neither desperate nor needy. If I lost the job over the circumstances in question, I thought to myself, I could live with that. The next day, I told the owners of the company what had happened first thing that morning (I wanted them to hear it from me first). The owners, a religious White couple, were concerned about what had happened. But, they understood. By lunchtime that afternoon, the guy had been fired and had already left town.

Recommendations/Resolutions/Lessons Learned
As a result of my life's experiences, I always ask myself what is to be gained (by both parties), and more importantly, is it worth it? Identify what the reason for the aggression by the other side is... what do they want from me? Most importantly, what is the power dynamic? If the power is on the other side, then I avoid escalation. What is the worst-case scenario? Is it worth it? That will usually give me a clear roadmap of what to do.

Racism poses some of the most challenging social situations to navigate in our society, as the natural instinct is always to "fight back." In fact, most of the Black kids I knew growing up, that's what their parents always told them - Fight back. In fact, some "demanded it," no matter what the situation was. "Fighting back" is just one skillset. Most people never understand that the best armies in the world operate on a principle of diplomacy 99.9% of the time. They actually never want to go to war. You only fight when you absolutely have to. Power imbalances reveal character. The greater the imbalance, the greater the reveal. Talk to people who don't look like you! Get their perspective on the world around them. Don't take off running to your sociopolitical comfort corner the first time you hear something that doesn't fit your worldview. Think for yourself (my father's words to me constantly as a young person growing up). Don't let the man on the AM radio dial tell you who to like and not like - or, who to hate (or Fox News for that matter).

Testimony #30
Title/Area of Expertise: Computer Scientist/Business Owner
I experienced instances where other employees were given better salary increases, and I had high-level performance reviews. I had vacation days cancelled for no reason and always had to be on call. They always monitored other coworkers I went to lunch with. It created a hostile

environment for me and I went to HR after my boss' behavior didn't change. The final time I went to HR, I left early and told them I didn't feel comfortable. The director of the IT Department called me at home and told me they were letting me go, and I could pick up my belongings with security by that Friday.

Recommendations/Resolutions/Lessons Learned
I filed a discrimination claim on that employer with EEOC. We had to go through mediation, and I learned that documenting everything is golden. Most people that are racist know they are. If possible, address them and tell them how and why you feel offended. Also, don't be naive into thinking your conversation is going to change their viewpoint. It's 2020, we are still dealing with systematic and blatant racism.

Testimony #31
Title/Area of Expertise: Retired Federal Employee
While working in the federal government, everybody knew when annual promotions would come around that one qualified Black person would be selected. It was sort of an unwritten rule. You could apply but we all knew the outcome.

Recommendations/Resolutions/Lessons Learned
None provided.

Testimony #32
Title/Area of Expertise: Entrepreneur
A colleague in the workplace continually disregarded and disrespected my working environment and posted offensive racist signs on equipment used for the needs of client services.

Recommendations/Resolutions/Lessons Learned
None provided.

Testimony #33
Title/Area of Expertise: Educator
Someone recommended that I go back to school so I could move up in the educational arena. So, I started an Ed.D. program with a white

counterpart. I finished before her, but she was promoted twice before me. Another colleague didn't have an MA or Doctorate degree but was moved to an administrative position with just as much money as I was making with my degree.

Recommendations/Resolutions/Lessons Learned
Does it pay for me to work hard and sacrifice time with my family? I do have pride that I worked hard and have been told my Doctorate will pay off.

A MOMENT TO REFLECT

Stop, relax, close your eyes, take a deep breath, reflect, and ask yourself the following questions…

1. Which blatant testimony stood out the most for you and why?

2. What was the lesson(s) learned, if any?

3. If you identified a blatant testimony that you related to, what could you have done differently?

4. Which person comes to mind when you identified with the declaration?

5. What is your plan of action to rectify this situation?

6. Do you believe it can be resolved?

7. Are you willing to pick up the phone, send an email or text message, or use a virtual platform to have an exchange of dialogue with the person?

8. Consider using the Shawn E. Model: "Close our eyes, take a deep breath, reflect, and recognize that everything will be alright!"

9. Consider relying on the model that Dr. Darlene V. Griffin Willis uses, which is God's scripture, "…quick to listen, slow to speak, and slow to anger" (See James 1:19).

10. Are you willing to try applying the Willis A^3 Model (acknowledge, accept, and apologize)? If the answer is yes…go for it! If the answer is that you are not ready…keep reflecting, re-reading, praying, meditating and searching to find the best resolution for you!

EMERGING THOUGHTS

Thoughts from a Black Man

"You ain't Black." This is a phrase that I have heard my entire life. A phrase that has confused, annoyed, angered, and characterized me. Equipped me. A phrase that has affected every aspect of my life. A phrase that I have come to loathe. A phrase that minimizes the potential and the possibilities of a human being. In the eyes of many, being Black can only mean one thing. If one is Black, you are loud, athletic, can dance and rap, eat certain foods, speak Ebonics, are fatherless, unpatriotic, dress gangster, use the N-word, have served time, and are poor, ignorant… ghetto. That is the definition of a Black man to many, but not to me.

Unlike real Black people, I grew up in a two-parent household. My parents hailed from Texas and Louisiana, both of Creole descent and moved to Southern California in their youth. Both are Black, but light skinned. Therefore, from birth in the eyes of many, I was not Black because my skin was not dark enough. My family moved to a Northern California suburb at the start of my elementary school years. Elementary school is where I first learned that I was not Black, where I first learned that if you were White you could be anything. If you were Black, there were limits, assumptions, and stereotypes.

I grew up in a beautiful town full of wonderful people. It was safe, quiet, wealthy, and highly educated. Locals identified my family as the "Black family that drove the Honda." The other Black family drove a Volvo. I think I was the only Black kid in my grade, well if I was "really Black." In elementary school, I first learned how different I was from everyone else. See, when you are the only Black kid you have the burden of representing everything "black." Magically, I became an expert on slavery, racism, and everything related to Black history. As a kid, I hated the month of February. The teachers never called on me on all the other months, but February was different. February was Black History Month. Moreover, who better an authority than me to talk about Black history? Who better to play Martin Luther King or Jackie Robinson in the school play than me? I did not know any more about Black history than anyone else in the school, but I looked like I should know. As early as second grade, I realized that I had the burden of representing all Black people. That ideology holds true still to this day.

As I got older, more and more students were vocal about their assumptions. I had to explain to them why my lunch looked similar to theirs. I did not have fried chicken and watermelon for every meal. My mom was capable of packing me a ham sandwich. My peers looked at me as if I were adopted, an intriguing outsider who curiously attended their school. They asked questions about how I cut my hair, do Black people have red blood, did my dad play professional basketball, and why did I move to their town? I had to defend myself for liking baseball, Billy Joel, history, similar movies, being articulate, and wearing a collared shirt. Collared shirts have been my uniform of choice since the seventh grade. My dad directed me to do so because he figured I would have a fighting chance against teachers, police officers, and parents with a collar around my neck. Maybe that collar would show them that I was not just another "Black kid." It could defuse a possible threat. Maybe that collar would provide me some respect in the eyes of others, or at least the idea that I was worth something. To this day, I am teased about wearing polo shirts. What people do not understand is that I still wear polo shirts to get respect, because without the shirt I am just another Black male. Well, if I were Black.

The trials and tribulations of my youth helped prepare me for life–life as a Black male in a White dominated world. Like most Black people, I have stories about being profiled, stereotyped, and subjected to outright racism. I also can tell you that most of the people I am closest with are White. From time to time, I am still told that "I ain't Black," even though life has repeatedly reminded me that I am. To those ignorant individuals who see Black in one prism, I feel pity. Their obliviousness to the world is a detriment to them and all of society. I know that I am Black, no matter what I choose to do.

"Black" comes in all shades–dark and light. Black is at a country music concert, an art museum, fine dining establishment, and golf course. Black is reading a book, a police uniform, or a corporate office. Being Black should not impose with it a character limit or a pre-determined life direction. It should not carry with it any additional burden. Individual citizens do not represent a race; they represent themselves. There are unlimited shades of White. It is time to recognize that the shades of possibility for Black are also infinite!

Thoughts from a Black Mother

This message touched my heart while reading some posts on my social media.

I woke up worried and fearful, even as a Christian with faith in Almighty God. I worshipped with a great online service with my church.

If I'm a believer, why am I so afraid?

My 36-year-old BLACK American son, who lives in Portland, OR, was about to go on a run as he does every day. We discussed the news of the day, especially of the clashes in Portland the previous night. I begged him not to go. When he said he was still going, I asked him not to leave his neighborhood and not to wear earphones so he could hear everything around him.

I can't believe I am here. Again. Still. Flashes of the "talks" of DRIVING WHILE BLACK. What to do if you get stopped at night on a different street in, yes, OUR suburban, upper-class neighborhood... and yes, what to do if you get stopped by police. NEWSFLASH: when Black, you don't have to be a criminal or do anything wrong to get stopped by the police. You can be lost in a neighborhood looking for your study partner's house, have a broken tail light, or driving a car you don't look like you should have, in a neighborhood you don't appear to belong in.
This is not hyperbole. It's real.

You see, I have friends and people I love, from many different backgrounds, races, and religions. I hope most would say that I haven't beaten them over the head about "poor me" and how "life is hard for my Black people."

I have it so much easier than most.

Here's the thing:
I don't want my son to be a statistic or a trending hashtag. I don't want him to be another Ahmaud Arbery for whom people will march or protest to ask "others" to care.

I worry that he will cross paths with a person filled with hate. (Yes, it is hate when an American feels like they have to jump in their car, flaunting their 2nd Amendment right, to hunt down another human being who doesn't look like they should be jogging in one's neighborhood.)

That person will see my 6'4" muscular son, but won't know (or care) that my son graduated from both Stanford and Pepperdine Universities, owns a home in Portland, has a wife and three little children, two parents who raised him, and many, many friends and family who love him. They won't care that he grows food in his garden, is a vegetarian, an athlete, and yes, a Christian.

Hate doesn't care.
I've been sick to my stomach and anxious all day.

By the way, I have another Black son who doesn't live in Portland, but whom I pray over every day with the same heart-pulling angst and concerns.

SHAWN E's STORY

Shawn Edward Washington, II had just turned 29 years old on March 30, before his passing on April 26, 2019. He was the only son and eldest child of my baby sister, Dianna, and had two younger adult sisters, Sheryle and Sharon. I am Shawn's aunt from his mother's side. His father lives in Ohio but had limited interaction therefore leaving him to be the young man of the house. Shawn lived with his mother, a single parent, and our parents. There are six daughters in our family, each a year apart. All of our names begin with D's so our Mom and Dad regarded Shawn E (what we called him) as the son they never had.

Shawn helped support his mother, my sister, who is disabled. He helped contribute to my parents' expenses as they all lived together, with the exception of his baby sister who got married to her firefighter husband four months after Shawn's death. In fact, Shawn was supposed to have the first dance with his sister.

Shawn was happy to be expecting his first child, Shawynce, who he never got to meet. His girlfriend was to give birth in July and unfortunately, she had to bring their daughter into this world without Shawn being present.

Shawn was loved by countless people. He was an artist, photographer, and videographer, in addition to working for Amazon where he was promoted three times during his first year. In addition, he worked as a camp counselor for the Catholic Youth Organization (CYO) where he counseled and positively affected countless children, especially those with special needs.

Shawn was a humble leader who loved helping others. He was a naturalist and a healthy young man who loved life. It is our view that the health system failed him. He checked into Kaiser around 1:15am, by ambulance, coughing up blood. He was declared dead at 8:21 a.m. that same day. Prior to that day, he went to Kaiser on April 2, a modern urgent care, and a dentist, but to no avail.

His funeral/celebration of life was full to capacity with over 800 family, friends, co-workers, and campers. In fact, his camp family also held a separate ceremony to honor his life and legacy.

He was truly an amazing young Black man that didn't have to die that day. The autopsy said the main cause of death was pulmonary hemorrhage and sepsis. When the medical records were reviewed, there were major inconsistencies.

The hospital didn't offer to do an autopsy. When we met with them, they kept apologizing, saying they would have handled things differently. On each of the hospital/facility visits prior to April 26, no one took blood tests. He didn't even get treatment for sepsis until later on, despite the test results being back earlier. Hmm, the life of a Black man!

Unfortunately, the facility was short staffed that evening and had to call personnel over from the hospital side around 5 a.m. but by then it was too late. Instead of moving him to the ICU as the doctor ordered, they moved him to a larger room in the ER where he was finally intubated and eventually died. The hospital took hours to confirm his insurance, despite him being in their database from a prior visit. It is our view that they were more concerned about his insurance status and the color of his skin than the seriousness of his condition and quality of his care.

We still do not know all the details affiliated with our Shawn E's death, as doctors and nurses have continued to tell inconsistent stories, none of which coincide with the medical records, which are also all over the place. We do know that the ER was very busy that night and EMT's were actively bringing patients in and out of the ER. It appeared that they were understaffed. The medical records don't even account in writing as to what took place during the last hour of his life.

It is our view that the death of our Shawn E, which took place on April 26, 2019, could have been avoided had the doctors, nurses, and staff adhered to the hospital protocols, treated him timely, secured his airways, practiced the ABC's of the emergency room, and treated him with quality care, despite his race and insurance status. He would still be here to raise his 1-year-old daughter whom he never got to meet.

Shawn E. continues to live on in our hearts and we often see his daughter talking to her Daddy as if he's speaking to her from afar. We feel him in the wind, we see him as orange butterflies continue to follow us, or as a fox sits "chilling" under a van. Often, we all stop in our tracks and whisper a prayer as we're reminded when the clock shows times like 4:44, 11:11, 5:55, etc.

Hospitals should be required to have enough staff and to take every case seriously, despite them being a Black male who had medical insurance with another company. Families should NOT have to be forced to find an attorney within a year's time only to hear countless attorneys say to you that, "Yes, we believe you have a case but the MICRA law doesn't allow us to seek the damages just to cover the defense." If you've never heard of the Medical Injury Compensation Reform Act (MICRA) of 1975 then please research it. This non-family oriented law was intended to protect the healthcare industries by lowering medical malpractice liability insurance premiums for healthcare providers, thus decreasing their potential tort liability. It defends the medical staff and hospitals instead of the victim and their families. If anyone has ever lost a loved one, it's no secret that you can't even say the person's name for at least 6 months and sometimes a year. However, if you want to hold people accountable, you must do so and the true current fact is you can't get more than the $250,000 cap on pain and suffering for cases involving medical malpractice. https://www.caoc.org/index.cfm?pg=issmicra

Don't get me wrong, it's not about the money, because it won't bring our loved one back. But it will help decrease the preventable deaths if we can "hit them where it hurts… their deep pockets!" We also want hospitals to change their policies, standards, and practices, especially when it comes to them treating Black people differently. We have proudly joined forces with the countless impacted families and lawyers who are working hard to change this law in California. Our goal is to get this outdated law changed by putting it on the ballot in 2021. Won't you please join us in this effort? More information can be found by visiting the Facebook page of Change4Shawn foundation.

As you can imagine, our family is devastated and will NEVER be the same! RIH our beautiful Shawn E. Wah, and know that your death will NOT be in vain. We will fight to hold those accountable for your death until we take our last breath and even then we will empower the grands and great-grands to take up the cause. Creating your foundation, Change4Shawn, is our commitment to make sure no other family has to go through what we went through at 8:21 a.m. on April 26.

We thank God for selecting us as family as we know that God's word says, "For I know the plans I have for you!" We are all here for a reason, season, and God's purpose! Well done, our good and faithful Shawn E. Wa!!!

WORDS OF WISDOM

Circle of Wisdom Advice

(Advice or stories from three seasoned Elders who continue to impact my life)

Seasoned Elder #1 - My mom and dad, who grew up two generations after slavery, gave me this advice and it's still applicable today...work hard, be compassionate and always truthful. Live below your means, avoid credit other than your mortgage or business, save at least 10% of your income and give an additional 10% for charity, church, etc. Don't let racial experiences distract you from meeting your goals and ambitions. Negativity may come your way, but if we keep God first, respect all people and their spiritual beliefs, then it will be okay. Stay positive, remember family, and know that nobody gives us anything; we must work for it!

Seasoned Elder #2 - I believe all of our young people need to have an awareness or knowledge that we have to be as good or better. We can't be classified as less...we have one chance to make a first impression! Presenting ourselves with dignity and respect is the key because if we don't then our intentions can be taken the wrong way. Make sure we understand the system. Put a mirror in our area and ask ourselves, would we hire this person? Know our rights and pursue the channels that protect us. We must learn how to navigate the system and always be ready for an opportunity. Lastly, ask ourselves what kind of person we are looking to model and be that person!

Seasoned Elder #3 - My mother was a school teacher and she taught my sister and me all the lessons we needed to learn about the difference between right and wrong. One of the most profound lessons I learned in schools and in life was that every human being is simultaneously like every other human being. We all share a common humanity. It is the things that we share only with some, not all, human beings that have bred an electorate polarized on almost every critical, political issue. A culture that used to respect, for the most part, the democratic exchange of ideas has been replaced with nasty, "over the top" rhetoric from both the left and the right. Each side claims that the other side is uninformed or misinformed. However, most often the case is ignorance on both sides of the broad range of consequences if their own position is embraced. There is a tendency on both sides to describe those with whom they disagree as evil, dangerous or even a threat to be eliminated. The evidence provided is usually questionable if tested by critical thinking. The danger of a Civil War appears to be well within the realm of possibility, this time with weapons that neither Grant nor Sherman could ever have envisioned.

My beliefs, attitudes and perceptions have been distilled over three-quarters of a century during which this country's tremendous commitment to freedom and justice compensates in large measure for those times that commitment was violated. Therefore, I have lived long enough to see how much can be achieved over the long haul. In a country where four of its first five presidents (and ten of its first 16) owned slaves, the American dream for many seemed more like a nightmare.

With that said, why should my history be of any importance to any of our fellow Americans? In 1944, Negro soldiers were dying in Europe but would be required to sit in the back of the bus in Georgia or Mississippi or Texas when they returned home a year later. Yet, I love this country every bit as much as some of our neighbors who today question our family's allegiance, our patriotism because we do not put a flag in our front yard on the 4th of July. The fact is that in 1944, in my segregated community, my relatives, including some returning soldiers, never burned down government buildings.

My neighbors, including skilled tradesmen, who could not join unions, never placed car bombs in front of courthouses, or disrupted the trading floor at the stock exchange. This must mean that they never saw that those injustices represented the essence of this country. In most instances, they chose peaceful demonstrations which did seem representative of the American way but were responded to with dogs, and tear gas, and bombs.

It hurts to read bloggers who do not protest when the police act unjustly but do if you don't sing-a-long with the national anthem. I really don't like the national anthem because those " bombs bursting in air" never seem to capture what I consider to be the essence of the nation. I'd sign a petition to have "America the Beautiful" become the national anthem in a heartbeat. Our country needs healing and if we all stay accountable and committed to speaking up when we see injustice then as the song says, "A Change Gon' Come!"

Nana's Story from a Grandson's Perspective

My grandmother Sheryle Marie Dyels-Griffin was born on December 17, 1942, in Berkeley, California. She has six sisters including a twin sister, Sharon, and two brothers who were all raised by Jake and Marion Dyels.

She grew up in South Berkeley, which was where most of the Black populous resided at that time. She, like my Papa, grew up with Black, White, and Japanese kids, speaking to the diversity of their upbringing. Although there was a friendly tolerance in the interactions of differing races, there was no (open) intermingling as far as dating was concerned. She does remember some secret encounters between races, but parents of both sides would not allow such open displays of affection to occur based off the societal norms they were raised under. Therefore, although she may have known and interacted with other races at school events, there were no interactions outside of the scholastic setting.

Nana describes the Black people of Berkeley as being in their own world, and would often mix into the White world out of economic necessity. Although she couldn't recall any blatant acts of racism, she certainly remembers the covert and subtle ways in which institutional racism reared its ugly face. For example, she explained that the White admin at Berkeley High would automatically place White and Japanese students into college prep courses, while Black students were almost always relegated to the wood shop or auto shop classes. Only a select few Black students would be sought after for college prep classes, further demonstrating the Willie Lynch practices of dividing Blacks in order to further entrench the stronghold of institutional racism rooted within the educational system.

Nana also described instances of colorism as being a prevalent piece of her upbringing. Nana inherited her father, Jake Dyels', hue. He was a Creole Catholic man from Melville, Louisiana. She remembers her skin color being an advantage for her sometimes as it related to her interactions with Whites. Her silky hair and fair skin often caused her to be mistaken for being a White woman. It worked quite conversely in the Black community. Nana described a time when a brother was attempting to win the heart of her sister Diane. Aunt Diane had introduced Nana to the young man as her sister, in which he replied, "This half-breed ain't yo' sister!" Nana laughs about it now, but she remembered these incidents of colorism being a trend in her upbringing and into adulthood. I find it appalling, that we still deal with these types of issues to this day! In 2020, colorism still plays a major role in the division of the Black community. It's a sad reality that we must tackle head-on in order to bring back a sense of unity within our community.

As Nana grew into being a mother, and began working side jobs to help support her growing family, she recalls an example of covert racism within the workplace. The year was 1963, and my mother Darlene V. Griffin at the time was a newborn. Nana's sister suggested a job at a dress shop that she had worked at. Nana was delighted to go work and earn extra money for the family. The job was going well, until the White shop owner suddenly laid Nana off. Nana decided to go down to the unemployment office to collect for the period of unemployment. The worker told Nana that her unemployment had been denied, because the employer had offered Nana another job. However, Nana explained that she offered her a job to clean the woman's house, and that she was NOT a housekeeper, but a retail worker! Subsequently, the unemployment office did their investigation and sided with Nana! This spoke volumes to me, because I know Nana to be a non-confrontational person, but she would not be taken advantage of. Her reaction to this form of discrimination was not violent or threatening in nature. She calmly explained the misdeed and the results worked in her favor. I know for a fact that her calm spirit and grandmother prayers have kept me alive on more occasions than I can count! It was refreshing to hear her demeanor being presented even in her younger years, and to see how it has manifested in her children and grandchildren.

This same soothing spirit would manifest another time, as she embarked once again in the late 1970s into the workforce. This time, a family friend, Ms. Green, helped her land a job as a teacher's assistant for the continuation school at Dewey High School in Oakland. She remembered the White teachers complaining when the Black female teaching assistants would take their breaks together. This meant that the fear stricken White teachers would have to deal with the Black continuation school students all by themselves. They could not control the classroom without the presence of Ms. Griffin, who would serve as a mother or auntie figure to the young Black males who were "acting out." Nana said that they would call their White teacher every name in the book, and all Nana had to do was give him a look and say, "Billie! Sit your butt down and relax!" Nana's soothing but serious demeanor would stop the coldest gangster in his tracks and he would reply, "Yes Ms. Griffin, I'm sorry." Nana observed that the main reason that most of these young Black men would act out, was that the teacher would force them to read. Since that elementary foundation was not established, they could not do so, causing them to act out with a sense of bravado or physical intimidation to detract from their illiteracy! She remembers having to review a list of "survival words" with them; words like EXIT, STAIRS, and STOP. These could potentially save their lives one day.

One chilling story from her days as an attendance clerk at Dewey was when she was feeling down, not having a good day. One of her students came in and said, "Ms. Griffin, what's wrong, you usually smilin', something is wrong!" She replied, "Just having a down day, nothing's wrong." He informed her that if anyone was messing with her, that he would ensure that they did not do so again! She assured him that she was fine, and didn't require his services. Come to find out, less than a year later, that same kid was arrested and charged with murder! This was just a testament to the type of love and respect that people have for my grandmother. They lived on 50th Avenue between Bancroft and East 14th, now renamed International Blvd., a notorious section of East Oakland. Their house was never robbed, shot at, or broken into, and all the drug dealers and gangsters knew and respected my grandparents and their house. Not only to the community, but to her family, she has always served as the voice of reason and a pillar of strength and wisdom to lean on. Nana always has a positive word, and will tell you the truth about yourself in the most loving and caring way!

Her advice to this generation is to think before you speak and act! So many times, she says, "Young people just act, without thinking of the consequences behind it." Nana stresses the importance of having a strategic reaction to perceived racism or disrespect. She is a Woman of God, so I will end with one of her favorite scriptures from the Bible that I believe exemplifies my grandmother's spirit of peace:

"Know this, my beloved brothers: let every person be quick to hear, slow to speak, slow to anger; for the anger of man does not produce the righteousness that God requires" (James 1:19–20).

Papa's Story from a Grandson's Perspective

My grandfather, James Cornelius Griffin, Jr., was born August 10, 1939, in Houston, Texas. He was raised by the late Reverend James Cornelius Griffin, Sr. and Geneva Verlena Griffin. He has one sister (Carriel), a beautiful wife (Sheryle Griffin), six beautiful daughters, eighteen grandchildren, and ten great-grandchildren. At the age of five, he moved from Houston, Texas, to Berkeley, California. By the way, my mom proudly carries the middle name of my great-grandmother and my brother proudly carries the middle name of my Papa.

He says that growing up in Berkeley did not present many incidents of blatant racism due to the city's surface reputation of having a liberal and diverse culture. As a child, Papa remembers having friends of all races. Nevertheless, by the time he was old enough to join the workforce, it was known that Black employees had to be better than everyone else to be considered for promotions. He doesn't recall many blatant acts of racism. However, one event stuck in his memory.

The year was 1945, and a 6-year-old James Cornelius Griffin, Jr. was with his family on a summer trip back to his birthplace Houston, Texas. He distinctively remembers the Southern Pacific train that he, his sister, and parents would board in Oakland. He remembered the decor of the train being nice and passengers sat where they pleased. All the normalcy of this American family vacation would be rudely interrupted when they left the seemingly progressive west coast for the stark southern reality of Jim Crow. Papa remembers that his family and the rest of the Black families aboard the train would have to get off of their cars and get on the back of the train as soon as they hit El Paso Texas, as the Texas border ushered in the government sanctioned Jim Crow laws. The fact that in 2020, my grandfather has stories of his experience in the American Apartheid is mind-blowing to say the least. He couldn't think of much advice to give to young people, due to the immense generational gap in societal norms and social constructs. However, he did reflect upon a time where children and young adults respected their elders and listened to the advice and gems they had amassed over time. Papa is not a very emotional or talkative man, but he says what needs to be said, and allows you to draw from it what you will. I think that is the lesson of his legacy; listen more than you talk, and when you do talk, speak with purpose and conviction!

A Dad's Story from a Son's Perspective

My dad, Phillip Willis, Jr., was born and raised in Jackson, MS. He grew up in the Jim Crow era and witnessed racism firsthand along with his parents and eight siblings. He learned early on that there was a place for Black people. Sitting in the crows nest to watch movies, drinking from "colored only" water fountains and being called the "N" word was everyday life. He didn't like it and worked hard to have a different life. He attended Jackson State University and became a member of Omega Psi Phi to help change the stereotypes affiliated with being a Black man in America.

Despite living his entire life under Mississippi's legalized apartheid, my father, like countless black men of the time, abandoned his personal goals for the shores of Vietnam in the name of the country that had barely recognized him as human, let alone equal. His enlisting in the Navy offered this Mississippi man a ticket to exotic locations around the world like the Philippines, the Caribbean, and of course, Vietnam. While the exotic foods, landscapes and culture were certainly exciting for the child of Phillip, Sr., who never left the state of Mississippi and Pernola, a devoted mother, wife and true Black queen, the scars this world tour of duty came with would last long after my dad took off the uniform. I do not have to detail it, but the "love for troops" that we now, rightfully, know as normal, was not extended to soldiers, especially Black soldiers, once they returned to the States. So after fighting for the country, witnessing sites unimaginable, my father and his heroic colleagues returned to insults and disrespect, along with limited to no resources to help heal their wartime traumas. Despite battling emotional triggers and bombs, to this very day, my dad did not let it stop him. After his work in the military, my father entered corporate America and quickly began his journey as an entrepreneur, importing goods from some of the exotic stops of his military days.

By the time my brother, three years older, and I were born, my parents began investing in real estate. This fruitful venture would prove to be quite the sound investment. Beyond its financial benefit, real estate allowed my parents, especially my dad, certain freedoms. Like the freedom to be a stay-at-home dad for many of my high school and middle school years. I could count on my dad to be home with an interesting news story, household chore or a lesson on memorizing the Greek alphabet, from a man of Omega Psi Phi's perspective, every day after school.

One of my dad's most memorable real estate transactions happened in the late 1990's. As I mentioned, my dad grew up in Jackson, Mississippi in the 50s and 60s, arguably the poster place for the Jim Crow South. Part of his childhood included embracing an early entrepreneurial spirit and mowing lawns in the neighborhood. I can only imagine the heat of the Mississippi summer sun beating down on his young black skin, as he pushed a lawn mower for acres and acres. Well, one of these hot summer days, after cutting the lawn of a long time client, my then pre-teen father, exhausted from his work, wanted to take a quick water break before continuing on to the next lawn. He politely asked, as my grandparents' upbringing allowed for no other way, asked his client for a glass of cold water. His simple human request was met with fear from his white middle-aged woman client. She hollered from a distance, "Stay right there! Don't you dare come in my house!" After a few minutes, the woman brought out a mayonnaise jar of water for my father to drink in the yard. Well, fast forward to present day; my dad not only still passes that house when we visit Jackson, he stops by to check on the tenants, as he now owns that very house. While I can say with great certainty that my dad will never live in that house, I know he has great pride in owning something that he was once denied access to.

That is just one of the stories of my dad's 70+ years on this earth. As a black man, he has witnessed, firsthand, some of the evils of this world, yet still finds a way to succeed, not only for himself, but his family. His time fighting these battles certainly has resulted in a few scars, but my dad is, and will always be my hero. His wisdom knows no bounds, his love, no limits and the lessons he has imparted will never leave me.

Blessed to call him Dad,

James C. Willis

CONCLUSION

Systemic racism is alive and well! The testimonies collected for this book are REVEALED and will affect countless folks for life! They don't just fade away but often keep us up throughout the night regretting how we reacted or did not react. I am thankful to God for waking me that June morning reminding me of this specific task!

It is imperative that we recognize that racism is NEVER okay and we cannot tolerate it! The difference is, instead of getting angry about it, let's be pro-active, bring it to light, and have a healthy exchange of dialogue. In fact, let's commit to following what I have called, "The John Lewis Challenge!" This amazing civil rights leader recently passed away and some of his last words to us were, "Answer the highest calling of our heart and stand up for what we truly believe!" I plead with each of us to take on this challenge and "get into some good trouble" for The Cause! We must all do our part and continue asking ourselves what else can we do? What else can we encourage our family and neighbors to do? I know what I'm going to do…

My response to the challenge is to make sure I **VOTE** on November 3 and in **EVERY** election thereafter! I've already completed the U.S. Census form and will continue to empower scholars and parents/families to navigate the educational system, making post-secondary success with attending and graduating from college the priority! What will you do to keep Congressman John Lewis' legacy going? I encourage you to post your response on your social media pages and tag #THEJOHNLEWISCHALLENGE.

My second challenge to all of us is to practice the Willis A^3 Model. It just may be the simple yet profound solution to help us begin healing our country! It requires all of us to take a deep breath, think about the challenge, then be prepared to <u>A</u>cknowledge (review the facts), <u>A</u>ccept (note what happened and that we can't change the past), then finally <u>A</u>pologize (it's not about who is right or wrong but being able to move past the challenge). We can take the first step by beginning to talk things through recognizing that we all may have played a role in the situation, but the good news is that we all have the ability to contribute to the healing process. Let's ask ourselves if the person dies tomorrow, would we be left with an unresolved issue or feeling better because we did our part to help resolve the conflict. The most challenging of the Willis A^3 Model is the apology, especially if in our mind, we have not contributed to the racial experience. It will take a mature person to apologize and perhaps being willing to not hear an apology in return. The ultimate goal is to not have any regrets but to begin healing broken hearts, misunderstandings and having a healthy exchange of dialogue which just may bring the necessary change for us all.

It is my view that we have more in common than we think. As a woman of faith, I encourage us to consider following what James 1:19 says, *"Be quick to listen, slow to speak and slow to anger!"* I'm talking from experience that this model is not always easy to follow but the more we practice, the better we become at putting it into action. We must talk through these challenges and, in some cases, agree to disagree with the outcome. Now let the healing begin!!!

TO GOD BE THE GLORY!!!

- Dr. Dary

ABOUT THE AUTHOR

Dr. Darlene V. Griffin-Willis serves as the Co-Founder/Executive Director of a family empowering non-profit titled, Concerned Parents Alliance and College Bound Programs. She served as an administrator at nationally recognized public and private institutions for more than twenty years and understands the importance of education, racial equity, cultural competence and being bold enough to have courageous conversations regarding racial experiences. Her comprehensive experience also encompasses partnering with an array of employers, school districts, schools, congregations, organizations and households giving her a remarkable knowledge base.

This first-generation college graduate and former PTA President has a successful record traveling around the country as a motivational speaker/facilitator utilizing a unique approach to reach her audience. Dr. Willis is a woman of faith who believes that she is following God's purpose for her life. She is also the co-author of the book, *Empowering Parents: A Guide to Taking Back Control of Your Child's Educational Journey* and the creator of "The Million Parent WAKE-UP Challenge."SM Dr. Willis is a proud life and 37 year member of Alpha Kappa Alpha Sorority, Incorporated.

This powerful orator not only establishes College Bound Programs, but she provides interactive workshops and keynote addresses to empower individuals and families. She is the creator of the "Scholarship Sundays with Dr. Dary" educational empowerment program and the Parent Express Educational Empowerment Programs (PEEEP).SM She coined the phrase, "Parenopoly,"SM an interactive and impactful series helping parents/families successfully navigate the educational system.

In addition to being an alumna of Harvard University's Management & Leadership Institute, Dr. Willis has an earned BA in Psychology from the University of California, Irvine as well as an MA and PhD in Organizational Psychology from the California School of Professional Psychology. This phenomenal woman was born feet first and raised with her five sisters in Oakland, CA. She is the proud daughter of James and Sheryle Griffin, the mother of two adult sons, Phillip III and James Cornelius, and resides with her husband of 33 years, Phillip Willis, Jr., in San Diego, CA.